THE CALL TO JUSTICE

Amos 1 to 9/Dorothy Harris

AN ALBATROSS BOOK

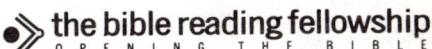

© Commentary: Dorothy Harris 1995
© Discussion questions: Albatross Books Pty Ltd 1995

Published in Australia and New Zealand by
Albatross Books Pty Ltd
PO Box 320, Sutherland
NSW 2232, Australia
in the United States of America by
Albatross Books
PO Box 131, Claremont
CA 91711, USA
and in the United Kingdom by
Bible Reading Fellowship
Peter's Way, Sandy Lane West
Oxford OX4 5HG, England

First edition 1995

*This book is copyright. Apart from any fair
dealing for the purposes of private study,
research, criticism or review as permitted
under the Copyright Act, no part of this book
may be reproduced by any process without
the written permission of the publisher.*

National Library of Australia
Cataloguing-in-Publication data

Harris, Dorothy
The Call to Justice

ISBN 0 7324 1022 3 (Albatross)
ISBN 0 7459 2453 0 (BRF)

1. Bible. O.T. Amos – Commentaries. I. Title

224.807

Cover photo: John Graham
Printed and bound by Griffin Paperbacks, Netley, SA

Contents

Preface		7
Introduction		9
1	A compelling relationship AMOS CHAPTER 1, VERSES 1 AND 2	27
2	Destructive relationships AMOS CHAPTER 1, VERSE 3 TO CHAPTER 2, VERSE 16	38
3	Relationship taken for granted AMOS CHAPTER 3, VERSES 1 TO 15	71
4	Relationships distorted AMOS CHAPTER 4, VERSES 1 TO 12	89

5 Relationships that sadden God
AMOS CHAPTER 5, VERSES 1 TO 17 — *108*

6 Relationships based on false hopes
AMOS CHAPTER 5, VERSE 18 TO
CHAPTER 6, VERSE 14 — *126*

7 The consequences of fractured relationships
AMOS CHAPTER 7, VERSE 1 TO
CHAPTER 9, VERSE 10 — *147*

7 Relationships restored
AMOS CHAPTER 9, VERSES 11 TO 15 — *174*

Endnotes — *185*
Bibliography — *191*

Preface

MY DAD WAS BOTH A POLICEMAN and a gaol chaplain. He used 'inside information' on the release of prisoners to collect them at their point of release before his colleagues could run them out of town or re-arrest them. He would bring them home and Mum would cook and wash for them. They would become part of our family, along with, at times, orphans and missionaries.

Mum and Dad refused to let any officialdom, church nicety or social priority challenge their care for the outcast. 'We did it because we loved Jesus,' they reflect now in their old age.

Gradually, I discovered that social justice was for many in the church more a point of contentious debate than giving drunks a bed and a meal at home. But a passion grew in my heart out of that same love for Jesus.

Several years ago, I was speaking at a seminar on God's heart for the poor. A church leader issued this challenge: 'Just where do you stand theologically?' Sensing his agenda to involve me in the social justice/evangelism debate, I closed off the discussion with, 'I just love Jesus.' But it is true. A vibrant love for Jesus was enough for St Francis, John Wesley, Mother Teresa. . . and my parents. Justice-making is only adequately birthed or sustained through a relationship of love with God. When this dies, justice becomes ideology.

Amos calls us to make relationships, not ideology central. He provides me with that firm theological basis for maintaining a lifetime passion for justice and the poor. He gives me courage to be less passive with evil, less afraid of oppressors. He provides assurance, too, that in working for justice for the poor I am participating in God's sovereign purposes as Creator. He is always wanting to restore, renew and transform. So I have hope for Cambodian orphans, Thai prostitutes, Australian Christians. It's a 'wild, outrageous hope', says Sine, 'premised above all on the love and faithfulness' of a God who is always longing to revitalise our relationships with him.[1]

In reading Amos, I have found Walter Wink's prayer helpful:

> God, help me to refuse ever to accept evil; by your Spirit empower me to work for change precisely where and how you call me; and free me from thinking I have to do everything.[2]

Introduction

FOR MOST OF US, the book of Amos has not been prime time devotional reading. A sermon on Amos is not regular fare. Many of us have heard that wonderful verse in chapter 5, verse 24:

> But let justice roll on like a river,
> righteousness like a never-failing stream.

Probably like me, you have found this verse profoundly comforting in its promise that justice is possible. Little did I realise that this verse follows one of the most powerful invectives on worshippers whose central focus is their own performance-orientated, smug complacency. It is meant to disturb, not soothe. It angered those who had opted for a self-serving system over a renewed intimacy with their sovereign God who could say 'No'.

Such love is demanding. Amos means to shock. He 'roars like a lion' (chapter 3, verse 8).

Amos was largely neglected by the ancient fathers, though reformer Savonarola preached vehemently on Amos and was executed two years later. It's risky to take Amos seriously! New commentaries on Amos proliferate. Since the 1960s, over sixty commentaries on Amos have appeared. Forty per cent of all commentaries published since 1800 have been on Amos.[1]

This prophet has become the favoured champion of the oppressed. Some who clutch onto him as an ally against injustice and alienation neglect the source of his inspiration: a vital relationship with his God. We tend to prefer causes to relationships, self-justification to humble repentance. Others shrink this relationship to a privatised ethic. But to Amos, justice flows out of transformed relationhips and involves the broad gamut of God's covenantal purposes — for society, for nations, for confronting the powers (seen and unseen), for the welfare of all peoples, particularly the despised.

To this prophet, the social is never reduced to the personal, nor the personal to the social. Amos' passionate commitment to justice is an expression of his relationship with God. It is so basic that some Christian leaders like John Perkins[2] claim such justice is God's *only* concern.

Amos and his times

His ministry probably lasted less than a year,

about 766 – 765 BC. Why such interest in a humble shepherd from the small southern city of Tekoa in Judah, between the desert on the east and hilly pastureland on the west? How did he develop such a sophisticated understanding of social, political, religious, *international* affairs as prophet to the northern kingdom of Israel?

The times of Amos were prosperous. Surrounding enemy nations, Syria and Assyria, were fighting each other, so Jeroboam II of Israel and Uzziah of Judah became strong. Their borders were extended (Amos 6, verse 14). Control over trade routes gave access to new wealth and luxuries. Amos' warnings of death and exile seemed very much out of tune. The rich felt secure with their holy heritage, genteel living, liberal morals, enthusiastic worship and contempt for the poor. To Amos, complacency and greed were not only souring life, but leading to destruction — rather an inappropriate and unbelievable message to the powerful who assumed life would go on, firmly in their control.

But it didn't. In 721 BC, only a few years after Amos, the Assyrians ravaged Samaria. Its population was massacred or deported and the northern kingdom was wiped off the map.

Amos' listeners had problems in taking him seriously. Seduced by their own power, they developed a theology to bolster their invulnerability. Loving relationships with Yahweh were mechanised into phoney systems in which their 'election' became a divine proof of racial superiority, sin was the deficiency they attributed to others, judgment meant the end of their vile enemies, righteousness became ritual correctness, justice secured the comfort of the powerful and Yahweh was a convenient tribal deity always on their side. Pawns of the state, cultic prophets gave these delusions social cohesion and moral rectitude.

Behind all of this corruption was a system of domination. Amos had been plunged into more than a 'flesh and blood' battle. Structures designed to care and promote faith had lost their divine vocation. They had become idolatrous. Subservience to the system dehumanised both the powerful and the weak. It was the powerful who must bear the responsibility for promoting these systems of evil. Only radical treatment could show them how deep was their enslavement. Only the Lord God, Yahweh, could liberate them. In Amos, Yahweh is always the creator, the initiator, the maker of history, the destroyer of nations — always longing to transform the old into the new.

Amos, who seemed so inappropriately gloomy, so southern, so *excessive* with such irregular theology, called for renewed relationships with a sovereign God who cared for all peoples, who would guarantee no immunity, who could not be manipulated by elaborate rituals or economic clout. To Israelites, opting for such a relationship in a world so tightly controlled and so nervously maintained seemed so slippery, so unpredictable, so free. Had not they achieved so much in such a hostile environment? How could their national security now be called idolatry, their worship sinful, their elegant lifestyles unrighteous?

The awful tragedy of Amos is that the people chose delusion over deliverance. Releasing control, becoming vulnerable, seeing God in others, depending on a relationship with one you can't manipulate — there was no future in this.

Exactly, said Amos. The God who gave you a past will not necessarily give you a future.

Amos' final cry is that there is always hope with the Creator. Yahweh is 'giving birth to a whole new order'.[3] But the birth process is painful for him and for his people. For most, continuing entanglement in current demonic strongholds was preferable to the pain of participating in re-creation.

Amos today

Few of us embrace pain willingly. We don't hear lions roar. Lions are more likely endearing toothless creatures like Wallace in that funny poem recited by Stanley Holloway about young Albert Ramsbottom's visit to Blackpool Zoo when Wallace spat the young fellow out because he thought it was Albert's birthday.

So lions don't really terrify us. We've learned to

dissipate our fears by making fun of them, domesticating them. We've probably never been scared out of our wits as Amos was on a lonely, dark hillside protecting the flock and his own life from an unseen lion attack. So for the word of God to grip us like a lion's roar is beyond our experience.

Just as we are not terrified by a lion, we are not likely to be gripped by issues of injustice. Generally, we are more afraid of higher taxes and bad cricket scores than about the impact of spiralling divorce rates or by the occurrence of injustice in our society. Further, we tend to be media-weary with images of famine and war. Bestial violence, though distasteful, is somehow more intrinsically intriguing.

Even when we are aware that our economic system is bolstered by trampling on the poor (chapter 5, verse 11), we can choose the security of concern from a distance. We might well like the idea of there being a river of justice and ever applaud the involvement of others in worthy, altruistic acts of sacrifice. However, our personal involvement is limited to money donations, sometimes generous, but sometimes also anonymous and superficial. Justice issues are often not integral to our faith.

Theologically, like the Israelites Amos was addressing, we have a God who is on our side. He will not say 'no' to us. The God who chose and who could also destroy is not our God. He will always comfort, understand, be there for us no matter what the situation. We're 'safe' in the new covenant. God will probably choose the soft option for us. There is a definite 'No' for the ruthless militarist (chapter 1, verse 3), the cruel slave trader (chapter 1, verse 9), the vicious human sacrificer (chapter 2, verse 1), but not for us.

We in the West enjoy the privilege of being the best-educated, the most healthy and the highest depleters of natural resources. The imbalance of the world in our favour may be unfortunate. . . but perhaps it is our destiny.

Will God roar 'No' at the very bases (religious, social, economic and political) of our lives? He did in Amos' time. God had little patience with power-wielding that led to crimes against humanity.

Affluence, both then and now, has not proved to be the enemy of religion — especially that type which emphasises fascinating eschatology (with an ever-changing kaleidescope of favourable futures for us), private spiritual 'highs', and escapist if appealing musical entertainment. It certainly sits well with polite but cosy lifestyles. But affluence is the enemy of developing intimacy with the One who calls for justice and righteousness, particularly for the oppressed.

Amos said all this (chapter 5, verses 21 to 23). But we find it hard to take him seriously. Judgment occurs to others, not to us. We are safe with our proof texts to guarantee this perception. It took a burning

Los Angeles, with the race riots that followed the trial of Rodney King's apprehenders, to convince some that US society could be brought to its knees. We could well listen more intently to modern prophets like Solzhenitsyn who said, at the height of the Cold War:

> The West is on the verge of collapse, created by its own hand. . . between good and evil, there is an irreconcilable contradiction. One cannot build one's life without regard to this distinction. . . We, the oppressed people of Russia. . . watch with anguish the tragic enfeeblement of Europe. We offer you the experience of our suffering; we would like you to accept it without having to pay the monstrous price of death and slavery that we have paid.[5]

This is disconcerting, but not terrifying because we have often forgotten that at the basis of God's judgment is the *abuse* of privileged relationships. Of those who have much, God expects much. He also judges societies. In doing so, he judges us as individuals because we inevitably contribute to the moral component of our local and national history, either actively or passively.

Amos is hard for us to take seriously today because we haven't realised how our faith has been captured by our culture. It is a faith that is highly personalised and privatised, with the healing of personal hurts and anxieties the key focus of growing

Western churches. We act as if economic superiority is an indicator of spiritual blessing rather than of the global trade imbalance, of which we are the prime beneficiaries. We rail against private sins, suggesting the powers of evil are limited to those agents of Satan we consider responsible for our personal inadequacies. We often lack awareness of our active participation in the more seductive systems of power and our complicity with cosmic powers which stifle the life-giving wisdom of God (Ephesians 3, verse 10).

We treat justice as an optional extra and still have endless debates on which is the priority: evangelism or social justice? We tend to take up sideline causes to protest against rather than embrace such central social issues as the denial of human rights. Our economic, our cultural, even our religious tradition anaesthetises us against the real issues on which our destiny depends.

We tend to be suspicious of prophets anyway, jaundiced by those modern proponents who are so excessive and flamboyant. We wonder whether people truly absorbed with a vision, ablaze for God, are indeed well-balanced. Like Amaziah in Amos 7, verses 10 to 13, we wonder if missionaries like Amos are culturally insensitive and should just go home with their bad news. The current solution to all ills is to be positive, not morbid.

An outspoken pundit commented recently: 'The

negative tone. . . has been a major cause of Australia's slow economic recovery. . . it is a case of ignoring the pessimists.'[6] We close our eyes in worship and the things of this world become strangely dim.

But Amos says: 'Open your eyes. Bear the awful pain of the ugliness of your niceness and your phoney piety.' What does he see today that we can't see? Does he see again a crumbling nation in the midst of prosperity — a people of God so full of ourselves that we can't care for others, let alone our nation?

At the basis of our current optimism is the conviction that, with enthusiasm, high technology and good management will win every time. We proved that in Kuwait in 1991, didn't we? — especially if we ignore the thousands of civil casualties and the devastated economies of many nations dependent on incomes generated in the Middle East. Let's focus on the *good* news. The church can be managed to succeed. Tyrants are defeatable. We have the blueprint for the millennium.

You are deceived, says Amos. This southern reluctant can't be dismissed as merely ancient. His vivid rural images may need translating for the modern urbanite. It may be more appropriate to compare the straining of God's mercy by sinners to the overloading of a soccer stadium at finals or to the pressure on the escalators at a retail store's sale rather than to the overloading of a cart (chapter 2, verse 13). But his message is hauntingly modern. The Creator has the final say.

Newsweek called 1992 the International Year of Fratricide — hate thy neighbour. Yet in *Newsweek*'s appeal to humanity, to be generous and caring to peoples less well-off, there was the caution to be wary of so-called open hearts which practise a new form of colonialism, a new white man's burden — not support, but self-interest; not liberation, but slavery.[7]

As in this case, journalists today are more prophetic than church leaders. Self-professed prophets in the church tend more to bolster up private visions than to unmask self-interest, duplicity and injustice.

Christians are in danger of losing their destiny as the people of God for this generation. The apostle James saw the prophecies of Amos as urgent guidelines for the mission of the church (Acts 15, verses 15 to 18). Christians today need to listen to Amos again — to renew their relationship with the rebuilder of the fallen, the restorer of the dispossessed, the One who gives his name to the disinherited.

'Prepare to meet your God, O Israel!' (Amos 4, verse 14).

Discussion questions

Talking it through

1 Do you believe that justice is God's *only* concern? What could John Perkins mean by this? If you disagree, what other concerns do you think God has?

2 Do you believe that God ever says 'No'? What does such a view of God indicate about the sort of person God is?

3 Do you believe our faith has been 'captured by our culture'? Expand on the following points made in the *Introduction* (pages 16 and 17):
  (a) 'It is a faith that is highly personalised and privatised, with the healing of personal hurts and anxieties the key focus.'
  (b) 'We act as if economic superiority is an indicator of spiritual blessing.'
  (c) 'We often lack awareness of our active participation in the more seductive systems of power.'

(d) 'We treat justice as an optional extra.'
(e) 'We tend to be suspicious of prophets anyway.'

How do you react to these statements:
- as new insights or old (leftwing) chestnuts? Do you think these statements are really accurate? Argue your case.

4 From this *Introduction*, how are you expecting the Book of Amos to affect you? Do you have the feeling that Amos is indeed a book for our times?

Widening our horizons

1 Do you believe that 'the imbalance of the world in our favour' is the developed world's destiny? In working out your answer, consider your response to each of the following:
(a) 'The poor nations have brought their suffering on themselves. They have a history of political corruption, under-development and personal laziness.'
(b) 'There are too many peoples who are poor for us to provide effective help. How can we tackle a problem like Africa? It's just too difficult.'
(c) 'We have worked hard for what we have. Those less well-off need to do the same — there is no instant, magic formula. Look at Singapore and the other young "tigers" of Asia.'

2 What is 'power-wielding'? What are some ways in which it manifests itself in:
(a) relations between rich and poor nations?
(b) relations between the privileged and under-privileged within the one country?

Why is God so strongly opposed to such power-wielding? What is the heart of his concern?

3 How can 'a new form of colonisation' towards poorer countries be avoided in each of these areas:
   (a) the provision of government aid?
   (b) aid from a non-government aid organisation?
   (c) the operation of multinational companies within a Third World country?

What are some practical, down-to-earth, *grassroots* programs that Christians you know have actually carried out? What was the project? What was the response? Did it work? Why/why not?

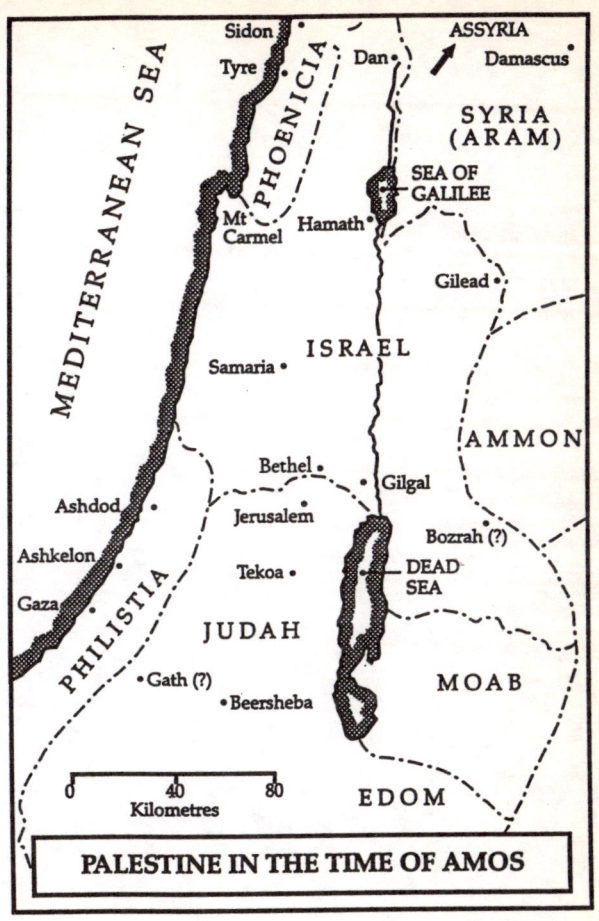

PALESTINE IN THE TIME OF AMOS

1
A compelling relationship

AMOS CHAPTER 1, VERSES 1 AND 2

'THE WORDS OF AMOS' (chapter 1, verse 1) seems a very ordinary, untheological introduction to one of the most powerful prophecies of the Old Testament and the earliest recorded prophet to Israel. But these words of Amos were the words of Yahweh who had irresistably grasped this southern shepherd from Tekoa and made him a prophet to the northern kingdom (chapter 7, verse 12). Tekoa was a fortified centre bordering the harsh southern Judean hill country about twenty kilometres south of Jerusalem. It was in the same general area where John the Baptist roamed and where Jesus was tempted.

Judah had been a separate nation from Israel since

the division of the kingdom after Solomon's death. The 'booth of David' (chapter 9, verse 11) was in tatters. The rival capitals of Jerusalem (in Judah) and Samaria (in Israel) vied for prominence. Israel definitely gained ascendency in Amos' time. A bitter religious tussle developed between the temple at Jerusalem in the southern kingdom of Judah and the altars at Bethel and Gilgal in the northern kingdom of Israel.

To the lordship of Yahweh, political boundaries and religious hegemony were irrelevant. To Yahweh alone Amos submitted, not to any state cult and its current king. Amos confronted this system of domination by showing it had no control over him.

'Amos' means 'the Lord carries' or 'the Lord upholds', reflecting that total dependence the prophet so desperately needed and demonstrated to fight this more than physical battle. This response of Amos' was the relationship God wanted of Israel — the only response God wanted to his long history of faithfulness to them. Justification of violence, manipulation of power, preservation of privilege at tragic cost to the poor, and racial superiority had become awful substitutes for these trusting relationships.

We may assume Amos was not from the elite. He may have had firsthand experience of the oppression of the majority poor in his own country which he condemned in the north (chapter 2, verses

6 to 8). Yet Amos' intelligent and broad-ranging appreciation of national trends and international crises suggest that he was more a herdsman (sheep-breeder and manager of a flock) than a shepherd, probably trading widely through both nations. Clearly, Amos had no personal ambition to be catapulted into confronting the sophisticated urbanites of the northern kingdom (chapter 3, verse 8). It had to be the call of God. Given his southern rural background, his prophetic calling was surprising: 'I was no prophet, neither the son of a prophet' (chapter 7, verse 14).

He made no apology for disassociating himself from the spurious prophets of the northern religious establishment. Perhaps long lonely hours of shepherding drew him close to his creator in uninterrupted communion. He retained a sharp observation and incisive critique which was not dulled by defending vested political interests, religious compromise and easy living. A refreshing amateur among staid ecclesiastics, Amos challenged, startled and disturbed those bogged down in slothful complacency — particularly, the high and the powerful. He unmasked the totally obvious and the fully denied. For such an uncomfortable role, the prophet had to be his own person, not beholden to anyone or any system. What else could sustain a calling demanding such focus, energy, rejection and pain, but an overwhelming encounter with God?

30/A compelling relationship

Amos only spoke what he 'saw' in a divine revelation (chapter 1, verse 1). Visions are the basis of his message (chapter 7, verses 1 to 9; chapter 8, verses 1 to 3; chapter 9, verses 1 to 4). Seemingly everyday events (locust plague, drought, plumbline, basket of ripe fruit) became authoritative revelations of his encounter with Yahweh (chapter 7, verse 1). Compelling judgments must be delivered to the people. Always the focus is not the prophet, but Yahweh, the sovereign yet compassionate one whom Amos had actually heard and seen and now must faithfully represent. The living God absorbed, controlled and separated Amos from others, but offered Amos no immunity from the consequences of being his mouthpiece.

Amos was a demanding, unswerving prophet at a time when there seemed to be little need for urgency. Under Judah's King Uzziah (792–740 BC) and Israel's King Jeroboam II (793–753 BC), both nations reached new heights of prosperity and security, though at the expense of others and their own poor. Israel, particularly, was basking in prospects of ongoing restoration even more glorious than Solomon's — as prophesied by Elisha and Jonah, Amos' predecessors (2 Kings 13, verses 17 to 19 and 2 Kings 14, verse 25). Surely, God was happy with them, thought the elite. They ignored the growing signs of decay in their nation and in external stability. They didn't expect an earthquake (chapter 1, verse 1) — recognised so often in Amos as a sign of God's judgment (chapter 2, verses 13 to 16; chapter 8, verse 8 and chapter 9, verses 1 to 6).

In fact, the chaos of the earthquake specified the timing of Amos' prophecy as accurately as possible — somewhere between 760 and 755 BC. God's word is always for a specific time: it is never vague. The earthquake introductory context fitted the God with whom his listeners were contending. He could shake the land so that it looked like the tidal Nile (chapter 9, verse 5). Yahweh was also the sovereign lion who roared and thundered (chapter 1, verse 2) in judgment.

Zion (chapter 1, verse 2) — the Jerusalem temple — was his true worship place, not the false shrines of Bethel, Gilgal, Beersheba (chapter 5, verse 5), Samaria and Dan (chapter 8, verse 14)). The word of Yahweh out of Jerusalem proclaimed his authority over all — from the lowlands ('pastures') of the south to mountains ('Carmel') of the north (chapter 1, verse 2). All who resisted would come under his judgment, described here as a pervasive, searing drought. Right up front, at the beginning of this book, the prophetic roar, awesome and dreadful, focuses on the key, twin evils of abuse of power and religious complacency.

Trusted relationships were abused and trivialised. The lion of glory was roaring in pain and anger at how his people could so totally pervert his purposes.

The lion must roar and roar through Amos.

How could Amos, an inferior Judean, express the uncomfortable mission God had given him to call all Israelites to repentance?

How could Amos counteract their calculating complacency — bolstered up not only by security and prosperity, but also by a theology that the Lord would always be on their side?

How could he convince them that their relationship with Yahweh was in tatters and must extend far beyond the performance of religious rites? Yahweh expected a commitment that touched every area of their lives. But they had twisted the relationship of covenantal love between two faithful partners into a mechanism of self-protection and exploitation.

How could Amos communicate God's reluctant yet inevitable judgment to a people who assumed they were immune?

Amos needed a strategy. With the consummate skill of the debater, his oracles were first directed at the surrounding enemy nations. Israel was used to interpreting judgment speeches against foreign nations as salvation speeches for themselves (see, for example, Isaiah 13, verse 23). So, these oracles would have been warmly received. Amos was preparing Israel for a devastating shock.

The shock will reverberate down to our times, too, if we will let it. For the task of the prophet has to do more with addressing the enduring crisis of all who claim to be the people of God, 'of having our alternative vocation co-opted and domesticated'[1] by the dominant culture with its 'economies of affluence, politics of oppression, religion of immanence and accessibility'.[2] Our task is to allow the specific crises of Amos' day speak to our own and to submit to the One who not only dismantles, but restores and energises.

Discussion questions

Talking it through

1 How do you see the book of Amos: as a social criticism text, a call to renewed relationships with God, or something else? What leads you to your conclusion?

2 What is Amos' impetus for involvement in justice issues? Is this still applicable to modern situations?

What are the dangers if this impetus is lacking?

3 To be realistic does not mean you have to deny the claims of transcendence. How do the apparently contradictory concepts of realism and transcendence fit together in Amos' thinking?

How do they fit together for us in a prophetic response to life issues?

Widening our horizons

1 'The essence of Christianity is not dogmatic systems of belief, but being apprehended by Christ. It is about a relationship with Christ, and all meaningful relationships involve risk. The true God does not give us an immutable belief system, but himself.'

Do you think this is the essence of Christianity? If so, how does it affect the way you live and the way you respond to others?

2 Comment on the following:

'The prophets,' says singer Garth Hewitt, 'were not commercial enough. They said things that were unpleasant.' Singers who focus on social justice issues are not very popular, either. But Christianity should have to do with truth and the truth is unpleasant sometimes.

In 'Broken Image', Garth Hewitt sings:

Come and walk the road with Jesus on the side of the oppressed.
Come and stand inside the kingdom

Where the story is redressed.
Come and stand with the broken,
Come and learn from the poor;
Take the side of the forgotten,
Let the image be restored.

('Lonesome Troubadour' album)

3 Who are the modern prophets? How do you recognise them? Would Cozzie qualify?

Cozzie (Fr Costello) heads up Rosie's Youth Mission at Surfer's Paradise on Queensland's Gold Coast. Not impressed by the beautiful beaches, the neon-lit hyperbole, the radio 'drivel' to con you into believing it's all excitement and fun in the sun, Cozzie openly curses Surfers Paradise as a modern Babylon on the brink of ruin. Schoolgirls moonlight as prostitutes, 250 street kids have nowhere to sleep, while luxury penthouses lie dormant — investments never seen by their owners.

Cozzie is convinced that if ten per cent of the money spent on golf courses had been spent on family support over the past decade, there would be no street kids. 'Forget about the beaches and the high rises and the hinterlands. It's people that count. If the community is not far-sighted enough to recognise the need to invest money in human infrastructure, in ten years time Pacific Fair (a huge shopping complex) will be a brilliant squat for kids.'

Entrepreneur Max Christmas is one of the priest's fiercest rivals. He wants the Rosie's team to move out of Surfers, a city he claims will become Australia's fastest growing town within two years.

Mr Christmas refers to street kids as 'rodents' who drift from one place to another like fruit pickers.

Four years ago Mr Christmas organised a free service with Greyhound Coaches to take the kids back to where they came from — something he says was short-lived, but successful. Mr Christmas makes no secret of his disgust towards the Rosie's team parking their buses in Surfers' mall. 'They bring the street kids into Surfers Paradise. It's like hanging out dirty washing in the main street on display for international tourists. They (Rosie's) are giving the place a bad image. You don't see people with their Hills hoists outside the front door of their homes. They hang their dirty washing in the backyard out of sight.'

Convinced that Surfers has been unjustly kicked to death over the past five years, Mr Christmas is heavily involved in the 'fix it' campaign with the catch-phrase, 'It's good to be seen in Surfers', set to hit the streets.[3]

2
Destructive relationships

AMOS CHAPTER 1, VERSE 3 TO
CHAPTER 2, VERSE 16

❦

Carol of the First Stone
*The woman's a harlot;
after we've thrown her
and known her and blown her,
we pick up rocks
in our sharp-fingered hands
and stone her.*

*Today it is day,
we sing the commandments.
Our children look to us
with the weight of their innocence.*

For their sakes, theirs truly,
we judge and apportion out
punishments justly.

> *The woman's a harlot;*
> *we have known her.*

The law is engraved,
who are we to dispute it?
Our children are threatened
if we falter in judgment.
For their sakes we sentence
the woman who sins,
the temptress who beckons.

> *And she is a harlot;*
> *after we've thrown her,*
> *we pick up rocks*
> *and stone her.*

We aim well; she will suffer.
We sing the commandments
and think of our children,
their trust and their innocence.
This Christ who rebukes us
speaks of our sins,

> *But we still have our duties.*
> *We stone her.*

'He without sin
let him cast the first stone.'
His voice is reproach —

> *we shuffle and frown,*
> *while she's off with a grin;*
> *though tonight if we're lucky*
> *we'll find her up town.*
>
> > *The woman was harlot;*
> > *we have all of us known her.*
> > *We shall pick up rocks*
> > *in our sharp-fingered hands*
> > *and stone her.*
> > *For him,*
> > *we shall stone her.*[1]

There is something in all of us that loves to see the guilt of others paraded and punished. We have a delicious tendency to judge, by our standards. Bad news about others is welcome, we reluctantly admit. Evil is fascinating. What we so stridently denounce in others is more than likely in ourselves, even in hidden form: 'No-one grapples with evil without contamination. . . The very sight of evil kindles evil in the soul,' wrote Jung. 'We are unavoidably drawn into the uncleanness of evil, whatever our conscious attitude.'[2] 'We have internalised the values of the domination system.'[3]

Amos called it sin. Israel recognised it so easily in others. She gave full approval to Yahweh's summons to the nations of Syria and Palestine. What a menacing roll-call: brutal Aram (chapter 1, verses 3 to 5); slave-trading Philistia (chapter 1, verses 6 to

8); treacherous Phoenicia (chapter 1, verses 9 and 10); carnivorous Edom (chapter 1, verses 11 and 12); bestial Ammon (chapter 1, verses 13 to 15); vindictive Moab (chapter 2, verses 1 to 3).

All merited the full force of divine judgment, including faithless Judah (chapter 2, verses 4 and 5), Amos' homeland. Israelites were appalled at such a despicable lineup. Amos had them agreeing with him. Wasn't judgment inevitable for those who had caused so much suffering?

Aram's armies had invaded Gilead (in Israel), grinding tortured prisoners like grain on a threshing floor. Philistia had captured whole communities of Israelites for their slave trafficking. Phoenicia was as untrustworthy as an ally as was vindictive Edom. What else but total judgment lay ahead for Ammon whose insatiable appetite for Israel's land made them stop at nothing, even ripping open pregnant women? Moab's contempt for Edom's dead did not injure Israel, but it was clearly contemptible.

All indictments are crimes, said Amos. Who against? God. On what basis? Israel's law?

No, said Amos. Even Israel would have agreed the norms for indictment were not those of their covenant tradition inherited from Yahweh by special revelation. Israel and Judah alone had the responsibility to honour these mandates (chapter 2, verses 1 to 3 and 6 to 12).

International ethics were not confined to their

covenant. These other nations stood accused by a more universal law of right and wrong, based on conscience, reflected in the nations' legal codes, international treaty rights and a common sense of morality. On these bases alone their guilt was beyond question.

To Amos, all sin is against Yahweh because he is the God of all nations. James Mays sums up this teaching in this way: '. . .international history is the theatre of Yahweh's dominion . . .patterns of events are an expression of Yahweh's actions. Yahweh himself makes history in a positive sense and cancels the history which men make in acts of rebellion.'[4]

Amos is implying that Yahweh is the accuser of the nations. Each nation is responsible to him, not to a foreign theology. As creator, he allows no human being to escape the obligation of being human. Even without special revelation, prophets or the written word, there is still a voice speaking within every person. Those without direct knowledge of God are still in relationship with him, as creator and sustainer of life. There is a 'law written on their hearts. . . their conscience also bears witness' (Romans chapter 2, verses 14 and 15).

Here, the focus of judgment is not the easily attested idolatry of Israel's heathen neighbours. The prophet clearly establishes the basis on which judgment could be justified in all societies — denial of human rights and decency:

People are not to be treated as things; human welfare has priority over commercial profit; promises need to be honoured; hatred promotes aggression; the rights of the helpless have priority over personal ambition; vengeance should be renounced.[5]

Societies which violate these principles stand condemned by the standards of all peoples. Underlying all of these is the Lord's concern for broken relationships, irrespective of whether the people worship him in recognised ways.

Amos was challenging the theology of his audience. Though all that he said in condemnation was familiar, it became alarming within this context:

* *All nations will be judged by the basic laws of humanity*. The source of these is Yahweh — the God of all the nations. He is not the preserve of any nation. No nation has the right to parade as the arbiter of others' moral standards, especially while justifying their own wickedness.
* *Whole nations are responsible*. All peoples are implicated in the sins of their leaders. Amos brought to biblical prophetic judgment speeches a powerful innovation, says Hubbard:

> Judgment speeches prior to his time were usually addressed to individuals (cf. Elijah's confrontation with Ahaziah, 2 Kings 1, verses 2 to 4). Amos directed them against whole

nations, demonstrating Yahweh's righteous concerns for international politics and human welfare.[6]

* *Accountability is proportionate to the knowledge of God's will.* Seeming advantages such as involvement in the covenant were not bargaining positions to lever more of God's favour.
* *History is always the acts of Yahweh*, not the external events of nations or of overpowering leaders.

The even-handed judgment of God falls on each nation in a judgment oracle. The prophet's logic is unavoidable. He is building a case to show how unnatural, indeed incomprehensible is the response of Israel to the God who is especially covenanted to them.

The common structural characteristics of the oracles

The common structure of these oracles against the nations with the repetition of various phrases creates an accumulative case that judgment is the only recourse for a morally responsible God. The common formulae and motifs fill out this international roll-call into a reprehensible union of flaunting authority.

1. *'This is what the Lord says'* (chapter 1, verses 3, 6, 9, 1 and 13; chapter 2, verse 14).

Called a 'messenger formula', this occurs at the beginning and end of most oracles (apart from chapter 1, verses 10 and 12). Here is the divine confirmation of the source and authority behind the prophet's words. It has the immediacy of a conversation just heard and reported.

There is no mere repetition of ancient texts, but the freshness of encounter with Yahweh himself. This is the decisive word which will determine the destiny of nations. It is not the manufactured spleen of a member of an enemy nation. The God of all nations is speaking. He will act in authoritative and specific ways.

This warning through his chosen prophet is not the mere babbling of his own words. How can Amos not prophesy (chapter 3, verse 8)? Ignoring the word of the prophet, the divine messenger, was a denial of their very life source (chapter 8, verses 11 and 12).

2. *'For three sins. . . even for four'(chapter 1, verses 3, 6, 9, 11 and 13; chapter 2, verse 1).*

This is a familiar literary device in wisdom literature to direct focus to the accumulated evil — particularly the last-mentioned vice, probably the most severe.

Some view the three and four as components of completeness, symbolised by the number seven throughout the Ancient Near East. The continuing saga highlighted by the form reflects the reality that each nation had sinned more than enough to warrant the Lord's judgment. Punishment was more than merited. There is no slight case against the nations, as indeed later there will not be against Israel.

Here, Amos defines what he means by sin. It is the arrogant denial of the authority of the sovereign Lord of all nations. Amos' audience heartily agreed that these nations were abject sinners. They had previously been under David's rule, but now were out of the covenant. As Walter Wink says: 'So they were sinners: racially impure, socially inferior, ritually unclean. Their actions demonstrated this, ran the twisted pop theology. They were 'victims of [the listeners'] oppressive system of seclusion. . . whose evil. . . [was]. . . ascribed to them'.[7]

Amos didn't absolve any of their responsibility, but his definition of their sin was different. They were sinners because of their rebellion and injustice, not because of their exclusion. This was a bitter lesson in theology for the Israelites, who claimed covenant immunity for similar evils.

3. *'I will not turn back my wrath'(chapter 1, verses 3, 6, 9, 11 and 13; chapter 2, verses 1 and 4).*
International crimes seemed to go unnoticed and the ruthless were unhampered by any accountability. The powerful always bulldozed themselves into immunity. Every atrocity seemed to get an unhindered 'yes'.

But the divine 'no' was coming. The heavenly warlord needed to respond to be true to his character of righteousness and justice. The judgment will be final and complete. He thunders, destroys, consumes. 'I will do it,' says Yahweh. The language is militaristic, plain and decisive. And it is always with fire. 'I will send fire' (chapter 1, verses 4, 7, 10, 12 and 14; chapter 2, verse 2) — the symbol of judgment particularly against the misuse of power and bestial inhumanity against the weak.

There is no reference to other gods punishing the nations. It is Yahweh alone who stands as protector of the weak and helpless, the establisher of justice, the judge of the powerful. Abuse of power is his chief focus — those leaders who put themselves above the universal laws of normal conduct — where might, personal gain, revenge and total devastation of the helpless become weapons to attain and maintain their authority.

Yahweh the judge and holy warrior alone is sovereign. His judgment alone, not wars, opposing military might or fate, controls the destiny of nations. These judgments of others lulled Israel into believing that the lion would never roar against them. Their day of the Lord would witness their brilliant rescue, they must have thought.

Distorted relationships of Damascus, capital of Syria (chapter 1, verses 3 to 5)

Many battles between the kings of Israel and the neighbouring kings of Syria took place in Gilead

— a sort of buffer zone for over a hundred years. Its rich pastures and woods were occupied by three tribes of Israel, but ripe for the picking at any point of weakness. Two Aram rulers focus the wrath of God in Amos' oracle: Hazael (c. 843 – 796 BC) and Ben-hadad, his son (c. 796 – 770 BC). It was their treatment of their captives rather than their invasions which incurred judgment.

Hazael was a particularly barbaric king, known for his brutality in Gilead. Captives were forced to lie on the ground while heavy iron threshing machines with sharp iron knives mutilated their bodies into a bloody killing field. This was gross ingratitude when Syrians had been treated generously by Israelites (1 Kings 20, verses 31 to 34; 2 Kings 6, verse 23). Even if 'threshing' is one of Amos' agrarian metaphors for inhuman treatment of war victims, fiery judgment was God's response. Further, Ben-Hadad contracted a brotherly covenant with Samaria (1 Kings chapter 20, verse 32) and then denied it.

Their magnificent 'fortresses' in verse 4 (referring to the fortress-like dwellings of the rich and powerful in Amos 3, verses 9 and 11 and chapter 6, verse 8) — symbols of their security won through unbridled arrogance and inhumane power-wielding — would be burnt up. They were an assault on Yahweh's sovereignty.

The gate of the capital of Damascus would be insufficient for protection. The fire would reach rulers in other areas (Aven and Beth-Eden). The location of these areas is disputed, but the sense is of thorough and widespread penetration of God's wrath into every area of wickedness (the valley of Aven means a valley of wickedness; Beth Eden means house of pleasure).

The final irony of their wickedness is that Syria was to be exiled to Kir, the uncertain eastern location from which they had migrated centuries before (chapter 9, verse 7). Yahweh was to act as judge on behalf of a people defenceless before invaders.

Distorted relationships of Gaza, capital of Philistia (chapter 1, verses 6 to 8)

The focus of God's judgment was then directed to this mighty southern nation closest to Egypt, another long-standing enemy of Israel. This further condemnation was welcome to Amos' audience in Samaria. The rhetorical pattern is predictable, developing the momentum that the only logical outcome is the fiery judgment of Yahweh.

Gaza here is the focus: a large sea port and junction of main trade routes. For economic gain, they made slave raids (probably on Judah and Israel) and forcefully dislocated whole masses of people, not just war victims (peaceful people is implied). Yahweh's reproach is against their using people as objects of merchandise with the Edomites.

For making themselves wealthy on the gains of

human trafficking, God was to see to it that all forms of security, achievement, human grandeur, ill-gotten power through force ('walls', 'fortresses': verse 7; 'kings', 'sceptre': verse 8) would be devastated. Ashdod and Ashkelon, strong fortifications north of Gaza with Ekron to the east, would suffer, demonstrating the thorough sweep of God's judgment. This judgment may have been the Assyrian invasion of 734 BC and forced exile in 711 BC, and punishment for revolt against Sennacherib in 701 BC. Outrageous inhumanity only deserved total destruction — even worse than Syria's. Master is added to Yahweh's name here to stress his sovereign power and authority.

In awful union, then, Syria and Philistia were to be destroyed as the main military thorns in the flesh for Israel. The trouble is that the insignificant as well as the important, the perpetrators of evil, were to suffer. Amos's audience again was further bolstered by their sense of justice — the destruction of their enemies.

Distorted relationships of Tyre, capital of Phoenecia (chapter 1, verses 9 and 10)

Amos then shifted his tirade to the north-west. Tyre on the Mediterranean coast was famous as a prosperous commercial centre with far-reaching trade. But what awful cargo! Tyre and Gaza were both involved in slave-trading with Edom. They not only sold slaves, but acted as a broker to pass whole communities of slaves on to Greece (Joel 3, verses 4 to 8).

The arrogance and callous pride made breaking of a treaty (based on friendship) of no consequence. The treaty partner in verse 9b is not specified. It may have been Israel (1 Kings 5, verse 2ff). But the issue is the betrayal of trust to those loyal to her covenant pledge. Untrustworthiness and infidelity added to the heartlessness of bartering in human lives. Tyre was to receive Yahweh's fire of judgment — again directed at her self-made, island impregnability ('strongholds', verse 10 as in verses 4 and 7) and haughty disposal of treaties and whole peoples. Nothing was secure against the fiery justice of Yahweh for those who denied human dignity.

The form of destruction may be war or invasion (as in 585 – 573 BC by Nebuchadnezzar and in 332 BC by Alexander the Great), but the agent of destruction will always be Yahweh.

Distorted relationships of Edom, the nation (chapter 1, verses 11 and 12)

Edom, to the south-east, is implicated in previous judgment speeches against Gaza and Tyre as a fellow slave-trader. It had a long history of hostilities with Israel stretching back to the division between Jacob and Esau (Genesis 25 ff), Edom's tumultuous ancestor.

Edom's sin was solving a problem by military aggression instead of negotiation within the agreed covenant. The 'brother' may have been Judah, with whom they had a long, violent history. Whoever it was, it is obvious that the bitter betrayal of trust had turned Edom into a wild beast, relentlessly raging and attacking with a voracious anger (verse 11b). The major Edomite cities of Teman and Bozrah would be no longer protective havens or launching arsenals of incessant aggression and duplicity.

The proud strongholds, again, were the target of Yahweh's desperate judgment. Their vitriolic hatred was to be more than matched by Yahweh's frightful judgment fire. Their only future hope lay in their incorporation with Judah (chapter 9, verse 12).

Distorted relationships of Ammon, the nation (chapter 1, verses 13b to 15)

Ammon, called Philadelphia in New Testament times, is now called Amman, Jordan's capital. It lay on the east of the Jordan between Moab (south) and Gilead (north) and once belonged to David's empire.

Amos, here, delivered a stinging indictment against the nation of Ammon who, with Moab, were the descendants of the incestuous drunkenness of Lot and his daughters (Genesis 19, verses 30 to 38). Relations with Israel were brutal on both sides. Constantly restless for expansion of its cramped territory, Ammon made military skirmishes into Gilead. Its brutality associated with its lust for power is the focus here.

The unbelievable savagery to innocent, pregnant women and their unborn children was a common ancient atrocity to subjugate enemies by terror.

With frightening military precision, God was to act against the capital Rabbah (verse 14a), the seat of perverse power. All security was to be demolished. Battle cries now were to be heard against Ammon — those terrifying yells of impending defeat.

The violent wind imagery commonly reflects assaults on a city, but may also refer to a *theophany* — a visit from Yahweh himself, who not infrequently appeared in whirlwinds (see Job 38, verse 1). Yahweh himself was to intervene and confront evil with his superior power. The scene was set for massive chaos and frightening assault.

Amos was building his case that history is a revelation of God (hinted at in chapter 1, verse 2 and developed more fully in chapter 5, verses 18 to 20). Leaders were to be held accountable for parading as determiners of destinies. Again, those who had heartlessly used power would be humiliated in exile (verse 15).

Distorted relationships of Moab, the nation (chapter 2, verses 1 to 3)

Moab to the south had been a vassal state in David's empire but, after the schism, it came under Israel's control. Later, Moab resisted and withheld tribute.

Of similar dubious ancestry as Ammon, they too would hear war cries — an appropriate judgment on their military aggression and disrespectful vindictiveness. They had violated the ancient code of war which stipulated respect for the bodies of royal enemies. Total destruction and desecration even against Edom, also capable of degrading their victims, far outstripped the norms of human decency.

Jewish tradition (Targum) interprets the reference to lime as the ashes from royal bones used to whitewash their houses. Other tradition also suggests that this burning would deprive the king's spirit of the rest obtained from a decent burial. Cremation was reserved for contemptible criminals (Genesis 38, verse 24).

Kerioth (verse 2) may refer to Moab's cities or to a major town, where Chemosh the god of the Moabites was enshrined. A fiery battle, probably a surprise attack with tumultuous screams and the trumpet blasts of impending disaster, was Yahweh's response. It was a fitting, murderous punishment for rulers and officials, who showed no mercy to their neighbour's leaders.

Although this oracle has no direct connection with Israel, Yahweh intervened because he cannot tolerate such inhumanity. Yahweh, here, continued to establish himself as the one whose standards must be observed, even by those who do not know his name.

Distorted relationships of Judah, the nation (chapter 2, verses 4 and 5)

Amos then focussed his attention on the geographic centre — his homeland, Judah. While the condemnation of annoying, foreign nations would have given Israel considerable satisfaction, the oracle against Judah, Israel's estranged sister nation, would have brought special delight. The prophet continued to lure Israel into the web of apparent immunity by focussing on the sins of others — now, inferior Judah. But there is a startling change of focus here.

The oracle form is similar to that of the other nations, but the indictment is very different. The infringement is not against a universal sense of morality, but against those divine revelations to guide the lives of God's chosen people: 'the law of the Lord' (the torah), 'his decrees' (verse 4). These were crimes that only the covenant people could commit.

The root meaning of 'false gods or idols' of verse 4 is 'to lie'. False prophets had deceived the people. For generations the people had chosen to live by lies, which brought about increasing perversion in all aspects of life. The lies involved idolatry, power-wielding and desperate bolstering of their despised national status as 'thistles' besides the 'cedar' of Israel (2 Kings 14, verses 8 to 14).

The torah was in tatters ethically, politically and religiously, because Yahweh was no longer their only

Lord. Rebellion had become an historical process — an endemic 'sin history' says Old Testament commentator David Hubbard, 'parallel to the salvation history'[8] of God trying to love his people back into covenant relationship.

Breaking this covenant was, then, far worse than Tyre's breaking the covenant of brotherhood (chapter 1, verse 9). The law had clearly spelt out the election privileges and responsibilities of God's covenant with Judah. Rebellion against a total commitment of love was then all the more inexcusable and reprehensible. The whole land was to come under judgment. The strongholds of the evil liars were to be destroyed (verse 5). Judah, expecting to be God's instrument of judgment against the surrounding heathen nations, was now to be subject to this same judgment. Even Jerusalem, the sacred city Zion from where God's word thundered (chapter 1, verse 2), was to be consigned to flames.

At the heart of God's covenant dealings was his sovereign electing love: 'the one nation on earth that God went out to redeem as a people for himself' (2 Samuel 7, verse 23). No other merit applied. It seemed impossible that Judah's tribes had allowed themselves to be duped by the lie that rejecting Yahweh's sovereignty did not cancel his ongoing protection. All who led the people astray and their duped victims were to experience the only response of a righteous God: judgment.

Distorted relationships of Israel, the nation (chapter 2, verses 6 to 16)

The case against Israel has been developing with awful inevitability. After all the judgment oracles against other nations, Israel would have expected an announcement of salvation, 'the day of the Lord', with victory over all these neighbouring enemies so obviously living in abject rebellion. Listeners would have assumed Amos was moving towards this.

Their hopes were bolstered not only by their current military security under Jeroboam II, but also by their long history of God's covenant promises so faithfully fulfilled in the past. They, of all tribes, had most claims to God's loyalty and protection (2 Samuel 7).

A terrible shock was in store. Israel was a sinner — in fact, a far worse sinner than the nations whose judgment she so readily applauded. The other nations were condemned for their perversions in international relations. Accusations against Israel were for sins against her own people, particularly for the oppression of the poor.

The same 'three-four' accusation formula is used, but her list of rebellion is much longer (verses 6 to 13). It is interspersed with a recitation of salvation history which had by now become a stinging accusation. Covenant privileges, meant to lead the people to fear and love God, had been perverted into power-wielding weapons to oppress and abuse the weak and poor entrusted to them to protect (Exodus 23, verses 3, 6 and 11; Deuteronomy 15, verse 1ff; Leviticus 19, verse 9ff).

God treated the poor as his precious creation (Proverbs 14, verse 31; chapter 19, verse 17; chapter 22, verse 22f) and his friends (Isaiah 29, verse 19). Prophets always came to their defence (Isaiah 1, verse 17; Jeremiah 7, verse 6; Micah 3, verse 1 ff). Yahweh's nature, his will and concern for justice, were the norms for measuring the life of Israel.

By Amos' time, the law had become a legalistic prescription easily manipulated by the powerful. The desires of Yahweh for intimate relationships with his people and with one another had been thwarted.

To be called sinners was a rude theological jolt to Israel. Sin was what they defined in others — the racially inferior, the internationally scandalous, the ritually impure. But, here, Amos began to explore the radicality of sin. Sin is more than a subjective state of guilt (as is often the modern definition). It is a deliberate choice to live under the delusion of human perfectability, of the invincibility of powerful, demonic complicity. It goes way beyond faults in individual morality to a commitment to systems of domination. These have such spiritual force that the voiceless majority readily acquiesce and the power-wielding minority unwittingly become their pawns.

When the upper class of Samaria showed their

contempt for the poor, they showed contempt for their *God*. As one commentary states: 'To outrage a man is to outrage God who stands behind him. This is what was to be so plainly revealed by the cross of Golgotha.'[9]

❑ *Israel's current social evils (verses 6 to 8)*
Israel's current social evils (verses 6 to 8) took on tragic and heartless pathos because of God's relationship with his people shown in his past acts of kindness (verses 9 to 12).

Israel was responsible for all these evils:

1. *Israel sold the poor (verse 6).*
Israel treated its own poor no better than Tyre and Gaza treated foreign slaves. They denied their own law which required them to take no interest on loans to the destitute as a response to God's care for them as slaves in Egypt (Exodus 21, verses 2 to 11; Exodus 22, verses 25 to 27).

Instead of allowing the poor time to pay off a small loan ('a pair of sandals'), rich creditors demanded immediate payment and showed no mercy, demanding the debtors be sold into slavery. They had forgotten there is no service of God independent of service to one's neighbour.

The Law always unites love for God with love of neighbour (Leviticus 19, verse 18). The magnificent kingdom of Jeroboam II was to be destroyed for neglecting this truth.

2. Israel oppressed the weak (verse 7a).

In their desire to get rich, the powerful walked all over the weak, despite God's call to protect them (Exodus 23, verses 6 to 8). They insolently misused the legal system to deny them justice and to deprive them of their rights.

Every difficulty was put in the path to justice for the weak, to restrict and manipulate them, probably to seize their land and then to rent it back at exorbitant rates. In Jeroboam II's rule, the rights of the influential always won over those of the little people. The powerful stood condemned by the covenant of love (Exodus 20, verses 22, 23 and 33), the basis of the legal system.

God always sides with the poor in their suffering.

3. Israel abused the weak (verse 7b).

The Law provided protection for household female slaves against sexual abuse (a type of residential prostitution). Father and son were forbidden to use the same woman (Exodus 21, verses 7 to 9). Here, the woman may have been a daughter-in-law with higher status than a slave. Her family loyalty was abused by her relatives — a perversion of a patriarchal authority that was meant to protect and nurture.

God is always outraged by such flagrant violations of his laws to protect those who cannot stand up for themselves. Actions against the defenceless are attacks on himself, his purity and his holy traditions — signs of his kindness to Israel.

Some overtones of Matthew 25, verse 40 are here exposed right in the bosom of the family:

> Whatever you did for one of the least of these brothers (here 'sisters') of mine, you did for me.

4. *Israel exploited the weak (verse 8).*
The garment here is used as security against a debt. Only the poorest of the poor would have had nothing but a garment to give as collateral. Legally, it should have been returned by nightfall (Exodus 22, verses 25 to 27). But frequently, the rich used these garments, as well as wine taken as fines, for feasting at cultic shrines ('beside every altar') instead of honouring their pledges to the poor. Worship became a parody of heartless self-indulgence when there was no attempt to reconcile their legal and economic lives with their spiritual life.

Worship and acts of injustice are incongruous. Note the irony of 'their God' (verse 8b). This was not worship of Yahweh, the God of justice, defender of the poor. This god belonged to them rather 'than their belonging to Yahweh'.[10]

❑ *Past acts of God's kindness to Israel (verses 9 to 12)*
To contrast the actions of Israel's unjust powerful towards the defenceless, Yahweh presented a resume of his own merciful deliverance: 'I destroyed. . . I brought you up. . . I raised up.' Israel was now put

in her rightful place — as the object rather than the subject of divine intervention. None of these evils would have racked her society, if her relationship with Yahweh had been in its proper order.

1. *God destroyed Israel's enemies (verse 9).*
It is surprising that conquest comes before the exodus (verse 10). The order of salvation history is reversed to emphasise the power of Yahweh whose relationship they were treating so flippantly.

'Amorite' is a general reference here to the peoples in Canaan before Israel occupied the land. Their awesome height and strength ('cedars' and 'oaks') were no threat to the mighty and complete power of Yahweh (fruit and even roots are destroyed). Yahweh himself destroyed them. The Israelites were living in a land conquered by a Lord to whom they still had to submit. He is in control of history and still destroys the strong who exploit the weak.

2. *God brought the Israelites out of Egypt (verse 10).*
How could they forget the exodus — the central gracious act of God's deliverance in making them a nation (Joshua 24, verses 5 to 7)? The shift to the second person 'you' makes the question all the more plaintive and incomprehensible.

Further acts of God's grace, protection and care in the wilderness and gift of the land, after such great struggle, made their current acts of rebellion all the more unbelievable. Again, the sole achievement in the exodus is Yahweh's.

3. *God raised up prophets for Israel (verses 11 and 12).* God had further shown his great kindness and sovereign authority by giving the nation spiritual leaders, the prophets. Then the Israelites had both his very word (through the prophets) and his deeds (the exodus) to verify his commitment to loving relationships. The Nazarites' call to holy and humble living had been lived out before the people (Numbers 6). Wasn't this true? Wasn't this another example of God's hand on the nation from the beginning?

The only way for the people to deal with the embarrassing uprightness of the Nazarites and other prophets was to corrupt them (get them to drink wine) and silence them. The people acted ('commanded': verse 12) as if *they* were in charge, not Yahweh. He ruled that no prophet be muzzled (verses 7 and 8) unless judgment was invited (verses 16 and 17). The seriousness of rejecting Amos' own prophecy is hinted at here.

The most tender gift of God's covenant love, his very word, was rejected. To what greater depths could the relationship between Yahweh and his people deteriorate? He, whose power is unlimited and whose will is sovereign, had to act.

❏ *God's punishment of Israel (verses 13 to 16).* His response is solemn: 'I will. . . ' (verse 13).

Terrifying military defeat (pictured here as an overloaded wagon at harvest cutting the earth) was to be the means of punishment. The God who destroyed the Amorites (verse 9) would now act against his own people.

For those whose theology had degenerated into an ideology of national superiority, this was unbelievable. The invader's name is not mentioned as it is ultimately God himself who will destroy. There may be reference to the panic of earthquake, the judgment Amos predicted (chapter 1, verse 1). Both harvest (chapter 8, verses 1 and 2) and earthquake (chapter 1, verse 1; chapter 8, verse 8; chapter 9, verses 1 to 4) are associated here in Amos with punishment. The powerful fall under his awesome terror. Flight is useless, even for the swift (verse 14).

A desperate rhythm develops as warriors, bowmen, infantrymen, horsemen lose their lives. 'On that day', Yahweh will not come as the anticipated saviour, but as warrior and judge (chapter 5, verses 18 to 20). All human power and falsehood was to be stripped bare.

This is God's word, said Amos. It will happen. Judgment for Judah (chapter 2, verses 4 and 5) and Israel had a different basis than that of the surrounding nations whose judgment was based on their commonsense exercise of international morality. Israel and Judah's degree of responsibility was higher, and flowed out of Yahweh's love relationships. They had all the benefits of God's word, deeds and

Destructive relationships/65

covenant commitment. Rejecting these meant rejecting him and his sovereign control over them.

They who had once been poor immigrants had now become the abusive powerful who violated the rights of the needy. The sovereign one who took on the cause of the poor and needy against the strong on the international level was to act no differently with his own people.

To Amos, Yahweh was no national deity, biased in favour of his own. He was the God of all peoples of the region. As he condemned their inexpressible cruelty to others, their passion to humiliate and to obliterate their adversaries, he condemned Israel's treatment of their own poor.

The chosen people would have been scandalised by the charge that they had no more hope of salvation than the surrounding nations. Their foundations were being exposed as myth, not theology — the myth of the 'domination system'.[11]

It was a radical exposé, but a necessary one, claimed Amos. It was only by acknowledging deep-seated evil, *equal* to that of their enemies, that the first step to renewing relationships could occur.

Discussion questions

Talking it through

1 Some of the questions of Amos' times are disturbingly modern. Talk these through, looking at both Amos 1 and 2 and our own time:
  (a) Is there a universal sense of morality?
  (b) Who sets the standards?
  (c) Is the notion of human liberty a Western invention?
  (d) On whose authority can we say the abuses in one country are worse than in another?
  (e) Are there 'Third World' and 'Western' brands of human rights or just 'human rights'?
  (f) Is the insistence on universal standards just another form of cultural imperialism, whereby we impose our notion of human rights on others with a different tradition?
  (g) Is resistance to protecting human rights based on the desire of autocratic regimes to maintain their oppression, or does it spring from deeper sources?

2 Discuss this statement as it applies to Amos 1 and 2 and to contemporary society:

> To reject the sacred is to reject our own limits; it's also to reject the whole idea of evil.[12]

3 'Privatised holiness' — to what extent was it a problem in Amos 1 and 2? To what extent is it a problem today? Compare this:

> The danger of Western Christians is not so much that they have ignored holiness, but rather they have privatised its meaning: obedience to Christ has occurred at the level of sexual, family and face-to-face relationships, but the master values and powers of society, education, politics and economics have been accepted and not explored to discover their demonic association. When this occurs, salvation becomes the unbiblical salvation of abstract, individual man and not historical man.[13]

4 This comment is from an Aboriginal woman:

> If you have come to help me, you are wasting your time. But if you have come because your liberation is bound up with mine, then let us work together.

How was the liberation of the Israelites bound up with that of others in Amos 1 and 2? Is this true for us today? How does it work?

Widening our horizons

1 In the Falkland Road district of Bombay, 8 000 prostitutes are packed. Here is the story of one of them:

Her story is typical. Daughter of a poor farmer in a hamlet three days' walk from Katmandu, Manju was twelve when her mother died. Unable to cope with three children, her father handed her over a few months later to two strangers: she thought she was going to Bombay to work as a housemaid. When the two men sold her to a pimp for $1 000, 'there was nothing I could do,' she says. 'I was trapped.' She is never allowed to set foot outside the brothel. Moreover, she is expected to repay her full purchase price. Rent, food and clothing are also deducted from her wages, so that seven years later, she is told, she still owes $300.

Helpless, Manju, like many in her profession, is resigned to her fate. Returning home would not be an improvement. 'Even if you work twenty-four hours a day in Nepal, you do not get enough to eat,' she explains. 'One can endure anything except hunger. If I were a man, maybe I would have committed murder to fill my stomach. But as a woman, I became a prostitute.'

It is a choice being forced upon too many. Along the highway of cheap love that now circles the globe, the cost in destroyed lives has become a blight to rival any of the depredations mankind has inflicted on itself.[14]

Who are the sinners in this story?

2 Read this statement by Fr Shay Cullen, a priest in the Philippines, about what he calls 'the miracle crusades':

> This is where the Fundamentalists fail utterly. They fail to see what Jesus was really about and how he opposed the whitened sepulchres and the brood of vipers that controlled the lives of the poor for their own selfish and greedy gain. The Fundamentalists preach a Bible message that is one of docility and unquestioning submission to deprivation, poverty and suffering in this world, to be content with a reward in the next. Usually, this has political connotations.
>
> We see Fundamentalist religion telling people to accept injustice as part of God's will and those who protest and rebel against the evil forces that crush the poor are falsely branded as evil communists. That is why Fundamentalism has been easily infiltrated and co-opted to the cause of preserving an unjust status quo in society.[15]

In what ways is our expression of faith an instrument of oppression?

3 Someone has stated: 'The church is summoned to be at the bleeding point of the world.'

How can your church accept this challenge:

(a) in its formal church program?
(b) in its encouragement of church members' everyday activities?

4 What is Mother Teresa's secret of combining a passionate faith with commitment to the poor? Read her prayer to find the answer (then pray it to let it touch your heart):

DEAREST LORD, may I see you today and every day in the person of your sick and, while nursing them, minister unto you.
THOUGH YOU HIDE YOURSELF behind the unattractive disguise of the irritable, the exacting, the unreasonable, may I still recognise you and say, 'Jesus, my patient, how sweet it is to serve you.'
LORD, GIVE ME this seeing faith, then my work will never become monotonous. I will ever find joy in humouring the fancies and gratifying the wishes of all poor sufferers.
O BELOVED SICK, how doubly dear you are to me, when you personify Christ; and what a privilege is mine to be allowed to tend you.
SWEETEST LORD, make me appreciative of the dignity of my high vocation and its many responsibilities. Never permit me to disgrace it by giving way to coldness, unkindness or impatience.
AND, O GOD, while you are Jesus, my patient, deign also to be to me a patient Jesus, bearing with my faults, looking only to my intention, which is to love and serve you in the person of each of your sick.

Amen.[16]

3
A relationship taken for granted

AMOS CHAPTER 3, VERSES 1 TO 15

Said Hanrahan
'We'll all be rooned,' said Hanrahan
In accents most forlorn,
Outside the church ere Mass began
One frosty Sunday morn...

...'It's dry, all right,' said young O'Neil,
With which astute remark,
He squatted down upon his heel
And chewed a piece of bark...

...'If we don't get three inches, man,
Or four to break this drought,
We'll all be rooned,' said Hanrahan,
'Before the year is out.'

In God's good time down came the rain,
And all the afternoon
On iron roof and window-pane
It drummed a homely tune...

...And every creek a banker ran,
And dams filled overtop;
'We'll all be rooned,' said Hanrahan,
'If this rain doesn't stop.'

And stop it did, in God's good time,
And spring came in to fold
A mantle o'er the hills sublime
Of green and pink and gold...

...'There'll be bushfires for sure, me man,
There will, without a doubt;
We'll all be rooned,' said Hanrahan,
'Before the year is out.'[1]

Prophets of doom like Hanrahan are tiresome. Unrelieved disaster is not believable. We laugh it off or deny it. We're mostly numb to talk of judgment and death. Things will work out, especially for the people of God. The future will be better than the past. We live as if there is no end to our current prosperity.

The task of the prophet is, as Walter Brueggeman said, 'to cut through the numbness, to penetrate the self-deception, so that the God of endings is confessed as Lord.'[2]

Here Amos used every rhetorical skill possible to plead, to trick, to reason, to cry, to woo Israel back into relationship with Yahweh.

Amos 3 to 6 is a series of oracles or judgment speeches distinct from the pattern of chapters 1 and 2, with the prophet pleading that Yahweh be taken seriously, through the commanding 'Hear this word' (chapter 3, verses 1, 9 and 13; chapter 4, verse 1; chapter 5, verse 1). The case against Israel intensifies as the issues of these earlier chapters are developed. The accusation is: Israel treats its own poor and helpless with the same violence with which the foreign nations treat other enemy nations.

God deals with all sinful people on the basis of the commonsense of right and wrong. But he was to deal with Israel according to her special privileges. The reality is, said Amos, that destruction was to come not only to foreign nations, but also to Israel.

But this seemed unbelievable. Would the God who chose Israel now reject her? Wouldn't the promises of land, children, wealth, protection — even the presence of God — last for all time (Genesis 12, verses 1 to 3; chapter 18, verse 18; chapter 24, verse 18)? At this stage of Amos' preaching, his audience was probably shocked, offended and anxiously marshalling their theological defence.

Amos was quick on the attack to argue skilfully that along with God's special relationship with the people of Israel came God's judgment. In fact, to assume that relationships based on God's grace would continue when the people had rejected God's ways was not only deeply irreverent and hurtful, but illogical.

With privilege goes responsibility (verses 1 and 2)

The strong imperative 'hear this' (verse 1) comes from Yahweh himself. This is a covenant lawsuit from the divine council itself.[3] Listeners would have then expected harsh condemnation. But the plea is tender, almost pathetic.

'We're family', said Yahweh. 'With you alone have I been intimate' (or preoccupied). He reminds the people of the great exodus triumph (verse 1b, as also in chapter 2, verse 10 and chapter 9, verse 7) and proof of his love and faithfulness.

'I have given you more attention than other peoples' (verse 2a).

Why is the exodus linked here with Israel's special relationship with Yahweh and, later (chapter 9, verse 10), used against them as a sign that they were no different from other migratory nations? In the preceding oracles and throughout his prophecy, Amos stressed that Yahweh is 'a world God, not a national God'.[4] All peoples are subject to his unconditional sovereignty. The focus must always be on him: he elects, he leads out, he protects. He also always challenges any self-exertion, self-security. There have been many experiences similar to the exodus, but only one Yahweh, only one redeemer.

These verses declare that Yahweh *did* choose Israel. He was in special relationship with them. But they had shifted the focus of the election onto themselves. In doing so, they reduced the creativity of intimate relationship into a formula for assured superiority, for immunity — for even condoning evil. Their religious, economic, social and political structures fortified this.

Relationships have always been slippery — mostly hard work demanding constant repair. Israel preferred to opt for self-centred manipulation rather than confront their own bent towards destroying loving bonds.

Amos challenged their basic misinterpretation of election and history: 'Their orthodoxy eliminated the dynamic of a trusting relationship and substituted a static, non-relational, guaranteed benefit.'[5] They assumed the privileges of the past were valid for all time and exempted them from judgment. God would forever be indulgent to their faults. They presumed their current prosperity resulted from God's favour. They had overlooked their responsibilities in covenant keeping. God's discipline, equal proof of his loving concern leading to restoration by repentance, became unacceptable.

The awful shock here was that the abuse of privileges exposed them to greater judgment. God had a right to demand obedience from his own people. Verse 2 starts with loving assurance, only to move on to an abrupt 'therefore' (verse 2b) to give the full weight of judgment for abusing the covenant.

Such responsibility is a law of nature (verses 3 to 8)

Obviously the protests to this strong link between privilege and responsibility were loud and forceful. Skilfully, Amos shifted tack to a series of riddles in the tradition of the wisdom literature, luring the respondent into the obvious answer, 'Of course not'.

Amos first established the cause and effect relationship in everyday events and nature. Then he applied this principle to God's action. God's cause (the lion's roar: verse 8a) must have an effect (fear) in the lives of the people. How can the one who hears God's word not prophesy (verse 8b)? This is obvious: it is rational.

So the message of judgment for God's chosen people does have a cause. Amos needed to take the people down this logical journey to get them to agree to what God has led him to say and be.

Now for the riddles. The riddles in verses 3, 4, 5a, 5b and 6a are harmless. The answer in each case is obvious:

Can two walk together continuously without unity? (verse 3)
Would a lion roar if it had no prey? (verse 4)
Would a bird be caught if no-one had set a trap? (verse 5a)
Would a trap spring shut if it had nothing to catch? (verse 5b)
Would the people be afraid if the battle trumpet had not sounded? (verse 6a, all NIV)

But the riddle in verse 6b is more ominous:

When disaster comes to a city, has not the Lord caused it?

This question would not have engendered such ready agreement. Wasn't God on their side? Would causing disaster be equally his work as creating welfare? Did they worship this kind of God?

This is followed in verse 7 by a dogmatic statement, not a riddle: 'Surely the Lord God does nothing, without revealing his secret to his servants the prophets.'

Prophets are Yahweh's servants. This verse justifies Amos' role through access to divine counsel. Revelation comes before action. Prophetic messages are true as later salvation history confirms.

The sequence then reaches its climax in verse 8 with the last two questions:

Can anyone not be afraid when the lion roars?
Can anyone refuse to prophesy after hearing the
Lord speak?

There is the clear and awful parallelism between the lion's roar and the sovereign Lord's words. This message of doom is from Yahweh. And the shock is that the roar is against Israel.

Images from the everyday life of the shepherd-farmer to urban crises are interspersed with proof of the legitimacy of the prophet's calling. Amos *does* hear from God (verse 7). Yahweh *will* bring disaster on his people (verse 6b). Amos *must* be true to his intimate calling and announce God's plans (verse 8b). The ultimate cause of political disaster *is* God, as chapters 1 and 2 establishes. The lion's roar *does* reverberate through the prophet's being (chapter 1, verse 2; chapter 3, verse 8). Disaster *is* coming (chapter 3, verse 5).

The people should fear and make all attempts to restore the closeness they once had (chapter 3, verse 3). Their election and experience of the exodus (chapter 3, verses 1 and 2) were powerful original demonstrations of the covenant between God and his people. But these had not guaranteed a continuing relationship.

Dead orthodoxy had been substituted for dynamic relationship, which has inevitable cause- effect repurcussions. The riddles highlighted this. To ignore the roar of the lion was to invite catastrophe.

God's judgment was to be obvious to others (verses 9 and 10)

The case is clear. The people of God were to be punished (chapter 2, verses 6 to 16; chapter 3, verse 2). God has no other choice in response to his character and his covenant. Neighbouring nations, whose judgment was based alone on the standards of international decency, recognised Israel's need for judgment, even apart from covenant privileges.

The rich and powerful (alluded to in 'fortresses') of Philistia (Ashdod) and Egypt are summoned in verse 9 as witnesses with the grandeur of a state visit to Israel. As barbaric slave traders (chapter 1, verses 6 to 8), they were hardly impartial. Their judging over God's elect was hurtfully ironic.

From their vantage point over the city of Samaria, they could see that the so-called glorious reign of Jeroboam II concealed intolerable terrorism ('great unrest': verse 9) and oppression of daily life. The wealthy ruled by brute force and depraved subjugation of the weak (chapter 2, verses 6 to 8). Israel had outstripped Philistia and Egypt in these crimes. As far as we can tell, the prophets were the first people in history to regard the nation's reliance on force as evil.

Through lack of integrity, injustice had become their natural response. 'They do not know how to do right' (verse 10). All that was acceptable according to Yahweh's norms, particularly here in the law and trades, had been polluted. Good had been turned into poison. They amassed wealth and prestige through violence and oppression. The products of looting, robbery or victimisation of others were so excessive they had to be stored in 'fortresses'.

Yahweh hated this expression. Fortresses symbolised not only the development of urban culture based on an economy of trade and capital, but also a discriminatory class system that was not part of Israel's society before. Mutual responsibility was displaced by rapacious greed, more like the Canaanite social system.

But here is no simple hostility by Amos against urban commercialism. The river of justice and righteousness had dried up (chapter 5, verse 24). Symbols of strength were monuments to exploitation. From the point of view of basic human justice, Samaria obviously merited the judgment of God.

How humiliating to have the judgment approved by these morally inferior, ancient enemies (Philistia and Egypt)!

God's comprehensive judgment against Israel (verses 11 and 12)

'Therefore' in verse 11 ties the Israelite city of Samaria's deeds to its doom. An end would surely come to oppression, because the Lord had spoken against Samaria. The rich inhabitants of Samarian strongholds, so successful at exploiting others, were to be overrun by the enemy.

Their economic and political security has been obtained at too high a price — the suppression of liberty and independence. The whole nation ('land') was to suffer. Large fortified cities ('fortresses') storing the plunder of exploitation would offer no protection. Hopes for the future to offer security would be dashed.

At this, there may have been more objections that deliverance not destruction was the destiny of the people of God. The Lord himself retorts that destruction is certain and will be total (verse 12). Here is the evidence — from a scene very familiar to Amos. Only a few scattered pieces were to be left, similar to a lion's attack on the sheep (verse 12). Only scraps of the elegant furniture of the idle rich were to remain — 'the tattered memory of lazy luxury on fancy beds.'[6] God's response to lives of robbery, violence and heartless indolence is clear.

There may be also here a reference to Damascus, indicating that Israel's plundering successfully incorporated the capital of Syria at this stage. The foe is not mentioned. It is generally assumed to be Assyria. But to Amos, Yahweh is the real foe against Israel. History is Yahweh's story, particularly here — the saga of judgment by the one who rules over all nations (chapter 9, verse 7f).

God's comprehensive judgment is even more obvious to others (verses 13 to 15)

The court-like summons, possibly again to Philistia (Ashdod) and Egypt (verse 9), is taken up more urgently. These foreign nations were astonished to see how Samaria treated its own people. Yahweh's name is expanded to include 'Lord God' and 'God of hosts' (verse 13) — ruler of all the armies of earth and heaven.

A warning from a God of such power and might must be taken seriously. Israel is referred to here as 'the house of Jacob', recalling their beloved ancestor's amazing encounter with Yahweh at Bethel. But Israel could no longer trust in her election (chapter 3, verse 2) or any religious or social structures. Bethel had now become a cult of spiritual perversion (chapter 7, verses 10 to 17).

'On that day' (verse 14), the day of Yahweh (chapter 5, verses 18 to 20), Israel's judgment would be complete. All symbols of hope in religion, the altar and the horns of the altar were to be violently destroyed. Clutching onto horns of the altar (verse 14) was the safe recourse of the person who fled to a city of refuge until found guilty (Exodus 21, verse 14). The Bethel shrine was to offer no such security. Not only the worshippers, but also the system of worship were condemned as illegitimate and impotent.

God is not only personally involved ('I will') in

the destruction of spiritual corruption (verse 14), but also in the condemnation of moral decadence symbolised in the multiple, opulent homes of the powerful (verse 15). In a society where the majority were poor and lived under oppressive extortion in daily life (chapter 5, verse 11), such luxury was revolting and could only lead to judgment. A bitter theme runs from house of Jacob, house of God (Bethel), winter house, summer house, house of ivory to house of destruction.

Yahweh is saying 'no' to rebellion and injustice. The sovereign Lord, not politics of expansion or economics favouring the few, is in charge of this nation's future. The only acceptable indicator of being his people is righteousness, both personal and national. All private sin had national consequences.

There is no national sin without national judgment. For when disaster comes to a city, isn't it the Lord who has caused it (verse 6b)? He will punish. He will destroy. He will tear down. Calamity will be his work. Israel will be held responsible for her rebellion.

Discussion questions

Talking it through

1 'History does not take kindly to the complacent winner.' How do you assess this after reading part of this *Time* essay and reflecting on this section of Amos?

'The world moves not like an arrow, but a boomerang.' Nothing captures the nature of today's uncertain world better than Ralph Ellison's analogy. Unfrozen after the end of the cold war, history is back with a vengeance — full of menacing whizz, its trajectory unpredictable, always poised to return to a starting point some thought it had left for good.

Optimists saw history proceeding along a straight line until it hit its target. Admittedly, it was tempting to take the apogee of Western power for the end of history. After all, the West now rules the roost as never before. Its economic and military might stand unrivalled. Most governments the world over practise — or at least pay lip-service to — Western ideas of good governance, i.e. liberal democracy. The World Bank and the International Monetary Fund play the part of modern-day conquistadors. In some former colonies, Western ambassadors rule like viceroys of old. Coca-Cola and McDonald's have conquered all but a few nooks and crannies of this world. In short, modernisation appears to equal Westernisation.

But history does not take kindly to the complacent winner. The West's victories abroad go hand-in-hand with domestic decline. Its civic bonds have weakened; its founding principles are being forgotten. Political leadership is conspicuous by its absence. The consensus on collective security has gone and military spending is declining dramatically even as the rest of the world erupts. Western economies stagnate, while the Far East sets the pace of development. Korean workers sleep on the factory floor to save commuting time; their European counterparts, as the story has it, also sleep on the factory floor, but during working hours. That old stalwart, the Protestant work ethic, is being superseded by the Confucian variety.

It appears that a blossoming civilisation contains within it the seeds of its own undoing. Like someone who has worked hard during his youth, the West is easing off, leaving the field wide open for the next batch of winners — a changing of the guard, as history has witnessed many times before. . .

As long as the global conflict was one of competing ideologies, the West fought on firm ground. Now that the conflict has become a cultural one, it finds itself on shifting sands. Like the Roman Empire, it makes the mistake of looking down on the challengers as technologically inferior. Like the Roman Empire, it is slow to grasp the nature of the threat.

Here the firm views that Mahatma Gandhi held on Western civilisation come to mind. Asked to comment on the topic, he replied caustically, 'Western civilisation? I think it would be a good idea.'[7]

2 What is a Christian view of patriotism? Examine this one:

True patriotism acknowledges God's sovereignty over all nations and holds a healthy respect for God's judgments on the pretensions of any power that seeks to impose its will on others.[8]

On this definition, at what points did Israel *not* show true patriotism in Amos 3?

3 What evidence is there in Amos that the people of God were addicted to consumerism? Read this:

The contemporary church is so largely enculturated to the ethos of consumerism that it has little power to believe or to act.[9]

Test this by applying it to:
(a) our attitude to our homes and personal possessions
(b) our reliance on private means of transport
(c) our equating of a quiet, non-assertive lifestyle with an inherently Christian one.

Widening our horizons

1 Would most Christians today be welcoming or cautious about seeing direct divine activity in the events of history or their daily lives? Why?

2 Read this story from Thailand:

WAN. Wan is not sure how old she is, but thought she was thirteen when her mother knowingly sold her into prostitution more than a year ago. Her life is spent in one small room and she is provided with adequate food, clothing and some medical care.

Every three months her father comes to visit her and arrange with the brothel owner to raise a further loan against payment for her services. She has no idea how many men she has serviced, but says she often has between five and ten per day. If she refuses to work, she is beaten. She has not been told if she has AIDS, but has many diseases and is often sick and in pain.

A 1990 survey of northern villages reported that of the girls under sixteen years of age who had been sold into prostitution, 63% were sold directly by parents, 21% by neighbours or friends and 16% by agents. Of these families, 42% had an annual income above the poverty village level. Thus, desire for material good and the 'good life' rather than true poverty may also be causes for parents to sell their children. Selling children was viewed by some helpers and researchers as 70% greed and 30% poverty.[10]

What insights does this give us on the relationship between poverty and greed? Who are equivalent victims in our society: street kids, homeless mothers, single unemployed males?

For those of us able to care for their children and to hold their family together, what duty (if any) do we have to those less fortunate? Should we jeopardise the physical, financial, emotional and spiritual welfare of our family for the good of those without such benefits? What *is* God requiring of us?

3 Ignatius of Antioch said: 'The greatness of Christianity lies in its being hated by the domination system (*kosmos*), not in its being convincing to it.'[11]

How do you assess this statement? What are the dangers of being 'convincing'?

4 Is there any such thing as 'private sin' and 'private morality'? In what sense does all sin have social and communal implications?

4
Relationships distorted

AMOS CHAPTER 4, VERSE 1 TO 12

Vesper-Song of the Reverend Samuel Marsden
by Kenneth Slessor

My cure of souls, my cage of brutes,
Go lick and learn at these my boots!
When tainted highways tear a hole,
I bid my cobbler welt the sole.
O, ye that wear the boots of Hell,
Shall I not welt a soul as well?
> *O, souls that leak with holes of sin,*
> *Shall I not let God's leather in,*
> *Or hit with sacramental knout*
> *Your twice-convicted vileness out?*

Lord, I have sung with ceaseless lips
A tinker's litany of whips,
Have graved another Testament
On backs bowed down and bodies bent.
My stripes of jewelled blood repeat
A scarlet Grace for holy meat.
> *Not mine, the Hand that writes the weal*
> *On this, my vellum of puffed veal,*
> *Not mine, the glory that endures,*
> *But Yours, dear God, entirely Yours.*

Are there not Saints in holier skies
Who have been scourged to Paradise?
O, Lord, when I have come to that,
Grant there may be a Heavenly Cat
With twice as many tails as here —
> *And make me, God, Your Overseer.*
> *But if the veins of Saints be dead,*
> *Grant me a whip in Hell instead,*
> *Where blood is not so hard to fetch.*

But I, Lord, am your humble wretch.[1]

Marsden, the 'flogging parson', the first evangelical Anglican priest to the New South Wales colony, is now an embarrassment to people of a similar faith heritage. How could such behaviour, longing for the violent destruction of those who were different (Catholics), flow from such missionary zeal?

Similarly in the time of Amos, the relationship between Yahweh and his people had become so distorted that oppression and violence became the order of the day. To rule over someone oppressively was a sign that an individual did not fear God (Leviticus 25, verse 43). His law not only forbade the oppression of the poor and needy (Deuteronomy 15, verses 7 to 18; chapter 24, verse 15; Leviticus 25, verses 35 to 43), but made generous provisions for their needs. Constantly warned against hardening their hearts, the people were asked to give generously out of thankfulness for their current blessings and for deliverance from past oppression in Egypt (Deuteronomy 15, verse 15).

This was the heritage of those called to be the children of God: thankfulness, generosity, care for the needy.

But up till now, Amos had only found oppression and callousness (chapter 3, verse 9). Wealth gained by exploitation (chapter 2, verses 6 and 7) was used to bolster social standing and ambitions of power.

God will act. The enemy will destroy fortresses — symbols of greed and exploitation (chapter 3, verses 9 to 12). No false securities will stand firm (chapter 3, verses 13 to 15).

'Hear this word' (chapter 4, verse 1; chapter 5, verse 1) . More accusing summonses sound from the holy, sovereign Lord to whom this indulgent oppression is totally scandalous. His holiness reminds them of what they could have been (Exodus 19, verse 6) if they had been faithful to their calling. For holiness is no private ethic. The holiness that John Wesley preached inspired the war against slavery and many inner city missions to the poor. It was a social holiness. In the preface to his *Hymns and Sacred Poems*, Wesley stated:

> The gospel of Christ knows of no religion but social, no holiness but social holiness.

But relationships are distorted as seen in the lives of the wealthy women (chapter 4, verses 1 to 3), false worship (chapter 4, verses 4 and 5) and ignoring past judgments (chapter 4, verses 6 to 13). God's agony is excruciating. He warns. He pleads (chapter 5, verses 4 to 7, 14 and 15). What more can he do, but act?

Relationships distorted by wealthy women (verses 1 to 3)

Amos has already established that ruthless exploitation of the helpless poor is endemic in Israel (chapter 2, verse 6f; also chapter 5, verse 11 and chapter 8, verse 4). Here, the darlings of the social set are under judgment.

This is no anti-woman tract to prove that women are the root of all evil. The summons is in masculine form (as in chapter 3, verse 1 and chapter 5, verse 1), implicating both genders in the scandal. Women of the day may not have objected to being called 'cows' when comparisons are made with the endearing terms of the Song of Songs (e.g. teeth like a flock of shorn sheep: chapter 4, verse 2). Today, the term sounds revolting. At least being called cows from Bashan made them *quality* cows! Bashan was the most fertile part of Gilead and its animals were known for their strength, fatness and fertility — as well as violence. These women of importance led lives of idle luxury and sensuality — the result of oppressing the poor to meet their own excessive desires.

Of course, these women, skilled in manipulating, could not be directly implicated in the injustice. Their 'lords' or husbands were the instruments of their petulant nagging. Through them, they wielded power in the corrupt courts and by exploitative commerce.

The use of a word that can mean 'lords' for husbands (verse 1) suggests some may have been concubines. Their continuous, selfish demands were nauseous. 'Drinks' (verse 1) may refer to the wine unjustly taken as fines from the poor (chapter 2, verse 8) or the gorging revelry of those who were callous not only to injustice, but to their own impending doom (chapter 6, verse 6).

The picture is of unceasing, self-indulgent behaviour to maintain their high social status. What they paraded as beauty and blessing (Psalm 73, verses 4 to 7) was more the ugly evidence of extravagance and oppression (chapter 2, verses 6 and 7; chapter 3, verse 8). Their affluence had not been caused by Yahweh, but was the result of superiority and power seized by flagrant injustice.

St Basil the Great echoes Amos. The failure to respond to the poor in St Basil's day was equally unjust:

> The bread which you do not use is the bread of the hungry; the garment hanging in the wardrobe is the garment of the one who is naked; the shoes you do not wear are the shoes of the one who is barefoot; the money you keep locked away is the money of the poor; the acts of charity you do not perform are so many injustices that you commit.[2]

God's condemnation is vehement. He swears 'by his holiness', committing his very character to his decision to judge. His majestic power and purity stand behind his word. The day will surely come (also in chapter 8, verse 11 and chapter 9, verse 13) with momentous reversals as outlined in chapter 5, verses 18 to 20. The women who treated the poor and even their husbands like animals will be shamefully filed into exile through the broken-down city walls, prodded and dragged like contrary fat cattle (chapter 5, verse 27). 'Hooks' (verse 2) may refer to the Assyrian invaders' ropes, with hooks attached to the captives' noses or lower lips.

Whatever the reality, the picture is one of ugly devastation: the atrocities on the wealthy and powerful are equal to those they inflicted on the poor. The city is destroyed (by invasion or earthquake); the fat cows are disgracefully thrown out in the unknown ('Harmon' in verse 3 is of doubtful location — possibly on the northern border of Judah in the Bashan range). One thing is clear: the women and the men of Samaria will be held responsible. Their future suffering will be more terrible than what they inflicted on the poor.

Relationships distorted by false worship (verses 4 and 5)

Amos expected the response of the people to his invectives to be the usual enthusiastic rush to the shrines to offer some sacrifices. They had to keep God on side and gain his favour to avoid his punishment — just in case Amos was right. Covenant relationships had degenerated into mere ritualistic manipulations.

The prophet here mocks with bitter irony these meaningless, indeed demonic acts of worship. He turns the priestly call to worship (e.g. Psalm 95, verses 1 and 6) into a sarcastic parody: 'Go to the shrines and sin and sin again.' Worship had become sinful because it did not lead to righteousness and justice (chapter 5, verses 21 to 24, 25 to 27). Worship multiplied rebellion.

Both Bethel and Gilgal (verse 4) were places of transforming divine encounters for Jacob (Genesis 28, verses 10 to 22; chapter 35, verses 1 to 15) and Joshua (Joshua 4, verses 19 and 20; chapter 5, verses 1 to 10). But they had become competitive foci of nationalistic fervour, harlotry and Baalism — all forms of idolatry.

But Amos' invective here rails that the very excess of their ritual had become idolatrous. It was zealous: sacrifices every morning were geared to gorging, not to repentance. Tithing was an ostentatious parade of flaunted wealth, the special tithe every third day instead of every year (Deuteronomy 14, verse 28; chapter 26, verse 12). They wrongly burnt the leavened bread (Exodus 23, verse 18) as a thank offering instead of eating it as a peace offering. Celebrating their own well-being, it was more like an exclusive gala barbecue, probably guzzling the extorted wines from the poor and lounging on their non-returned garments (chapter 2, verse 8).

Their real motive was clear — self-promotion, not love of Yahweh. Amos makes it clear that the sacrifices are the people's idea ('your sacrifices': verse 4b) aimed at pleasing themselves, not God. His satirical call to worship became another form of judgment on Israel. To seek Bethel was definitely *not* to seek Yahweh!

Relationships between the people and Yahweh had degenerated into such arid formalism that they thought they could manipulate Yahweh with excessive 'spiritual' activity and paraded zeal. Their worship had nothing to do with God, his character or his law. Later, God will tell them how obnoxious he finds this flurry of religious activity (chapter 5, verses 21 to 24).

Today, we still get caught up in competitive and self-designed religious performances. The real purpose of worship is to help us to meet God. He is not present at events of paraded spirituality where there is no repentant humility (see also Isaiah 29, verse 13; Matthew 6, verse 1ff; chapter 15, verse 1ff) and no concern for the poor. 'Without right heart preparation, there can be no meeting with God.'[3]

Ardent zeal, even liturgical correctness are not enough. The cults of Bethel and Gilgal had broken with Yahweh because they evaded rather than enforced the Lord's rule over the nation. They flourished on an affluence gained by violence against the poor (chapter 2, verse 8). They produced a passion for themselves, not for justice or righteousness (chapter 5, verse 24).[4]

Relationships distorted by ignoring past judgments (verses 6 to 12)

The people's relationship with God was so distorted that, even with the increasing intensity of the calamities, they could not hear the loving call of God to his people.

'Yet you have not returned to me' (chapter 4, verses 6 and 8 to 11), the cry after each calamity, are not the words of a vindictive tyrant, but of an agonising father, who wants to lead his children back to himself to resume their relationship in which he is truly the sovereign partner. Their repeated decisions not to 'return' — not to *repent* — are extremely painful to Yahweh, as are his acts of judgment.

These were days of prosperity and increasing international success. Prophecies of future doom (such as chapter 1, verse 1) or reminders of past disasters did not shake the people out of their hardened moral and spiritual complacency. Their willing submission to systems of control was complete. Israel could not possibly be under God's judgment — so thought the upper class who were busy amassing wealth and cultivating ritual precision at the shrines.

Arrogance had blinded them to the spiritual dimensions of so-called 'natural phenomena'. God said plainly that he engineered every disaster: 'I gave. . . I withheld. . . I struck. . . I sent. . . I overthrew. . .' (verses 6 and 7, 9 to 11). He is the sovereign ruler.

This salvation history contrasted starkly with the philosophy of the official cult and its promises of security and blessing. There are always problems when history is diverted into philosophy. As French theologian Jacques Ellul says:

> God does not reveal by means of a philosophical system, a moral code or a metaphysical construction. He enters human history and accompanies his people. . . [His law does not]. . . fall from heaven. . . It is given in the course of an election and liberation as the attestation of a covenant. It cannot be separated from this series of events.

The law is the point of the covenant and the starting point of a new history.[5]

Like all human histories, there is no ready system of answers. But the religious cult of Amos' day provided watertight interpretations. They did not listen to Yahweh's interpretation of Israel's hardships in Canaan. So they could not recognise in all these blows the personal overtures of Yahweh.

As David Hubbard writes:

> Here, divine judgment in its varied forms is pictured as an expression of grace that should have induced Israel to repent, turn back to God and trust fully in him.[6]

But returning meant agreeing that the evil they so readily recognised in others was in them and controlling their most favoured systems of power — the courts, the cult, commerce. To choose faith was to opt for vulnerability and care for the poor. It was to opt for no set answers, but for a companion on the journey and for mutuality with other pilgrims, even those from other nations.

But the journey had become too risky, the evil too close. They choose the unreality of the delusory cult rather than risking the unpredictable relationships of faith.

1. *The Israelites ignored famine (verse 6).*
Famine is described as lack of bread or 'cleanness

of teeth' (NRSV). The date and nature of the famine are uncertain. In many biblical accounts, God used famine for his purposes (e.g. Leviticus 26; Genesis 41, verses 57 to chapter 42, verse 5; 1 Kings 17, verses 1 to chapter 18, verse 1). Yet the people still had no desire to do the will of God.

It is clear the famine did make them turn away from their oppression of the poor (chapter 3, verse 9 to chapter 4, verse 3) and ego-centric ritualism (chapter 4, verses 4 and 5).

2. *The Israelites ignored dought (verses 7 and 8).*
Lying between the desert and the sea, Palestine often misses its winter rain. Lack of rain just before harvest was devastating to farmers. When rain came, it was intermittent, so people had to travel from town to town to get enough water for survival. Even though they were exhausted and never fully satisfied, they did not cry out to God.

Later, Amos describes another famine and drought (chapter 8, verses 11 and 12), causing even more desperate and extensive searching.

3. *The Israelites ignored crop failures (verse 9).*
Blight, caused by a blasting hot wind or mildew or a plague of locusts, added up to enormous devastation. This may have driven the people to further ritualistic contortions, but they avoided any real encounter with Yahweh.

4. *The Israelites ignored military defeat (verse 10).*
Plague associated with military defeat was likened to those in Egypt. But this time the plague destroyed Israelites, not the enemy. The devastation of war, the putrid stench of decaying bodies of their elite troops — even of animals — caused no softening towards Yahweh.

5. *The Israelites ignored near destruction (verse 11).*
Almost complete destruction of some cities (perhaps by earthquake: chapter 1, verse 1), as happened so suddenly in wicked Sodom and Gomorrah, provoked no acknowledgment of God's grace. Like Lot and his daughters, they were literally snatched from the fire.

Again, Amos stressed, their hearts remained hardened to God's chastising through all these calls for renewed relationships with his people.

The inevitable consequence of distorting relationships (verses 12 and 13)

Because of this repeated lack of response, Yahweh called for a face-to-face confrontation: 'Prepare to meet your God' (verse 12). There are overtones here of the Sinai experience (Exodus 19, verses 11, 13 and 17). What should have been a positive process of being transformed by God's glory became an experience of terrifying judgment. They had to make themselves ready to deal with Yahweh in all his holiness and majesty — a frightening prospect after their relationship had been so severely distorted by the exploitation of the wealthy (verses 1 to 3), egocentric religiosity (verses 4 and 5) and deliberate ignoring of previous judgment warnings (verses 6 to 11).

The people would not return to him, so Yahweh would come to them. It was an unavoidable encounter (verses 1 to 4).

Amos then reminded his people that the awesome God they sang about was about to confront them (verse 13). This was not the first time Amos had called them to worship. In his satirical call (in chapter 4, verses 4 and 5), Amos had taken a familiar litany from the priestly tradition and used it against the people to mock their false religiosity.

Here, he goes to a well-known hymnal (chapter 5, verse 23). He also uses hymns (in chapter 5, verses 8 and 9; chapter 9, verses 5 and 6) following the announcements of Yahweh's personal, direct intervention. This is the call to worship truly, not to parade self-centred excesses as at the Bethel and Gilgal shrines.

In these three hymns, Yahweh is always creator. Only he can make things new. Only his magnificent power can move against the sinful 'dominant reality' to create hope beyond judgment, justice instead of injustice.[7]

In this particular hymn in chapter 5, verse 23, Yahweh is shown as the God who:

*   moulds the mountains as easily as a potter

* creates the wind
* declares what he is thinking to those who will listen (chapter 3, verse 7)
* terrifyingly turns creation into destruction
* comes in judgment ('treads the high places') to shatter symbols of prideful arrogance and false worship (as at Bethel and Gilgal).

Yahweh, the Lord, the God of hosts, creator, revealer and divine warrior (see also chapter 5, verses 8 and 27) must be encountered in worship.

Many commentators say these hymns are out of place or later additions, different in style and theme from the context. While there may be validity in some of the textual criticisms, true worship is always disturbingly inappropriate in a church wearied by self-seeking and serene in its cultural captivity.

Doxology is consistent with prophecy because, if separated from it, prophecy withers or becomes ideology, says Brueggemann.[8] Praise is the call to principalities and powers to abdicate all pretensions at absoluteness,[9] says Wink.

Worship restores wholeness. It is the sign of hope. It is the cure for the apostasy of the powers.[10] It's the opposite of seizing control. Praising is looking at the reality of Yahweh ruling in all sovereignty as true God. It reminded the Israelites that God had ruled right throughout their history of salvation and that any usurping of his dominion was temporary as well as futile.

The tragedy is that praise has been captured by a privatised, soothing spirituality. We can sing the words, but there is no energising for change, no incorporation into the only One who can create a new people out of deadened, self-serving pleasure-seekers.

Worship is meant to disturb, not soothe. Encountering the magnificent God of this hymn should have engaged the worshippers immediately in critiques of their own motivations, lives and social structure. How can we worship such a transforming God and serve so ardently the systems which are the antithesis of his righteousness and justice?

Doxology — the hymn of praise to God — is the ultimate challenge to those who want to manage and control:

> Only where there is doxology is there any emergence of compassion, for doxology cuts through the ideology that pretends to be a giver. Only where there is doxology can there be justice, for such songs transfigure fear into energy.[11]

It is obvious that the people here treated magnificent doxologies as self-securing jingles. Nothing was transformed — neither their calloused hearts, their injustice or the majority downtrodden poor. The Lord God Almighty could not continue his creating and revealing through them, but he would not withhold his destroying ('turning' and 'treading').

Discussion questions

Talking it through

1 In a patriarchal society like Israel, it seems obvious to blame the man for the state of society in verse 1. Why focus on the women here? What does it tell us about the *shared* nature of sin in human relationships?

What would be an equivalent situation today?

2 Compare Amos 4, verses 4 and 5 with Matthew 6, verses 1 to 18. What did Hosea say about worship (Hosea 6, verse 8)? What did Micah say about worship (Micah 6, verses 6 to 8)?

What do you consider are the main elements of worship?

3 Is worship only meant to soothe? How often does our worship disturb?

Widening our horizons

1 Consider this statement:

> Conservative Christians of a Western heritage usually believe that the primary task of the church is to seek and to save the lost — the personal salvation of individuals. Although in a sense society is redeemed when individuals or society are delivered from the domain of darkness, the task of the church must never be solely limited to personal evangelism. Since Satan has invaded the very fabric of society in the principalities and powers, messengers of God must not only redeem people from the strongholds of the principalities and powers; they must also challenge principalities and powers who have a grip on institutions and structures of society.
>
> Therefore, social action against a range of social evils including poverty, racial discrimination, bribery and drugs is a necessary part of bringing all things under subjection to Christ. In the sense that Christians are active in breaking the grip of Satan upon culture, the church must be made up of social activists.[12]

Is this a fair analysis of the problem and the solution? Do you agree with the above writer's comment that 'A prophetic call must ring out to bring God into powerless religion.'[13]?

2 The role of God in history is sometimes difficult to recognise. What do you see as definite lessons and possible lessons that God is seeking to teach us in each of the following:
(a) Slavery in the US up to the American Civil War
(b) The Holocaust
(c) Communism in the USSR, 1917–1989?

3 What do each of the following contemporary situations of social declension indicate about the extent to which 'the lessons of history' have or have not been learnt:
(a) The ethnic conflicts in Bosnia?
(b) The endemic famine in the Sudan?
(c) The disposal of nuclear waste?
(d) The homeless on the city streets of Western democracies?

What are the lessons of history in regard to each of these? Do you see history's value primarily as to teach us something about God or something about ourselves?

4 'Every newspaper headline is a call to repentance for those who have eyes to read it there.'[14] How do you view natural or man-made disasters — as unfortunate accidents, cruel fate, or the rebuking hand of God?

5
Relationships that sadden God

AMOS CHAPTER 5, VERSES 1 TO 17

ISRAEL WAS IMPERVIOUS to Yahweh's call to transformation in worship, so Amos continued to denounce their sins: oppression of the poor and self-centred religion. But the tone in this chapter is one of pathos (verse 2), insistent pleading (verses 4 to 7, 14 and 15) and stark announcements of judgment (verses 10 to 13, 16 and 17).

In all of this, we see a prophet struggling to give hope as he passionately pleads with the people. Yet the passage begins and ends as if it is all over.

The obituary of Israel (verses 1 to 3)
Amos calls the people to attention as he had before

(chapter 3, verses 1, 9 and 13; chapter 4, verse 1). This time he laments the death of a precious loved one. This is the obituary of Israel. It's over. The nation is dead.

'The language of grief is the ultimate form of criticism. . . for it announces the sure end. . .'[1] of the existing power system. Amos is alone in his lament. So his grief is multiplied. His only hope is that 'the ache of God'[2] could penetrate the numbness of their delusion. His pathetic sobs blurt out that the once mighty and beloved people have been totally abandoned ('fallen': verse 2). The tragedy is immense.

'Virgin Israel' (verse 2) increases the sense of useless loss and lack of fulfilment. There is an allusion here to the violation of rape by the ruthless invaders against 'maiden' Israel. The very land (verse 2b) which was the promised gift to the fathers and the symbol of Israel's fulfilment is now the scene of her death ('deserted'). 'The gift of blessing becomes the site of the curse.'[3]

The prophet's listeners, bolstered by the nation's obvious economic prosperity and military might, must have found his pessimism totally unfounded. They were not ready for a funeral. Everything that meant security for them was to die. There was no hint of any invasion yet. But the armies of Israel have already been decimated, says Yahweh (verse 3). The nation has no future. Yet even in the few left ('a hundred. . . ten') there is a slight reason to still have hope. God is still loath to bring total destruction.

A plea from God (verses 4 to 7)

The offer of life in verse 4 ('seek me and live') after the funeral lament (verses 1 to 3) reflects the paradox of the prophetic vision that flashes dramatically from the future to the present: only out of weeping comes newness. It is Yahweh who has spoken — the future has as good as happened. Do something now — weep and seek me so you may live.

Seek means 'turn to, be devoted to'. Israelites were used to going to the sanctuaries to worship Yahweh. They were zealous at this devotion. But here Amos gives them an astonishing and ghastly alternative: seek Yahweh and *live*; seek the shrines and be *destroyed*.

The form again is of a priestly instruction, but the officiating clergy is Yahweh himself. He offers himself to the people, pleading with them to choose life. The shrines of Bethel, Gilgal and pilgrimages to Beersheba in the south offered a cheap, hollow grace — in fact, death through the delusions of false promises of life and security. These shrines and their devotees are destined for exile and worthlessness (chapter 3, verse 14; chapter 5, verse 5). The call is to distrust religion that panders to the masses and bolsters their complacency.

'Gilgal' and 'exile' (verse 5) have similar phonetics in Hebrew. Bethel (house of God: verses 5 and 6) will become a house of trouble, perversion and idolatry for 'the house of Joseph' — a synonym for Yahweh's people (Joseph was the father of the two chief tribes of Israel, Ephraim and Manasseh). Religious rituals would provide no immunity against the fiery judgment to come, just as it didn't in the Assyrian invasion and in Josiah's reforming purges (recorded in 2 Kings 23, verses 15 to 18).

Yahweh is the only hope.

The hearers, probably pilgrims to these shrines, would have been shocked to hear this. All of their religious efforts amounted to destruction, not protection — an unquenchable fire, the same punishment as that recorded in the oracles against the rebellious nations (chapter 1, verses 4, 7, 10 and 12; chapter 2, verses 2 and 5).

The real motivation of their worship was exposed. They were not seeking God, but seeking his approval (chapter 5, verse 6). His promises and blessings were more important than his presence in their daily lives and worship. Ritual was designed to symbolise reality, but it so easily became the reality itself and led to mechanical performance.

But why did God reject all their fervent endeavours, the 'seeking' at religious shrines? The lack of justice and righteousness is the key (chapter 5, verse 7). 'If your worship was true,' says Yahweh, 'the quality of all your relationships (to me, to family, to law, to business, to the poor) would reflect your covenant with me and indeed my character.' This is best summed up in the combination of justice and righteousness (in chapter 5, verse 24; chapter 6, verse 12).

But Israel's response to God did not reflect these norms of the covenant. In their relationships with the poor, they turned the welcome news of justice into bitterness like poison. They hurled to the ground like rubbish the righteousness that God counted precious. God's covenant priorities were distorted.

Verse 7 highlights the amazing patience of God who still called for his people to turn to him (verses 4 to 6), despite their deliberate distortion of covenant relationships.

Justice and righteousness are almost synonymous when paired in Amos. They take us way beyond the legal requirements of the law. Central to his prophecy, they are comprehensive terms representing Yahweh's will for his people.

Justice is the primary term and means 'seeking or loving good' (chapter 5, verse 15a) — in other words, 'fidelity to the demands of all relationships':[4] king in relation to subjects, judge in relation to complainants, family in relation to tribe and relatives, community in relation to the suffering and the alien and all in relation to the covenant God. Justice has its source in righteousness (chapter 6, verse 12b).

In Amos, the setting for justice is the courts at the city gates. When the innocent are vindicated and the wicked found guilty, justice is done. But the duty of the court was not to administer an 'impersonal, objective, even-handed justice'.[5] It was redemptive, protecting the just — particularly the weak and poor — who, with no power or influence, could not maintain their rights apart from the justice of the courts.

As Stephen Mott writes:

> The task of creative justice was to restore the poor to their position of independent economic and political power in the community.[6]

Righteousness in Amos is not merely an absolute ethical norm. It is a term describing the relationships expected of Israel society. It represents the quality of life to be demonstrated by those who live up to the principles of the covenant. Righteousness was the basis of relationships: between Yahweh and people (demonstrated in the religious cult) and among one another.

The two were intensely intertwined. Yahweh was the initiator and sustainer of all relationships. The righteousness of each person contributed to the quality of relationships and was intended to reflect always that intimate union with Yahweh. Imbalances in relationships were to be restored through the courts (justice) and in worship.

The faithfulness of our sovereign creator (verses 8 and 9)

Amos then breaks out into another well-known hymn of praise to Yahweh, the sovereign creator (cf. chapter 4, verse 13; chapter 9, verses 5 and 6).

Again a hymn seems out of place sandwiched between bursts of continuing invective (verses 7, 10 to 13) against the people's distortion of justice and righteousness. Yet it is the faithfulness of God the creator that is celebrated here — at once powerfully energising, yet critiquing the people's current unfaithfulness.

In this hymn, Yahweh is the God who:

* is creator
* made the planets
* rules over day and night
* created the seas
* sends the rain
* is a God of war, of history
* destroys powerful systems
* overturns the strong and seemingly invincible.

The hymn provides a startling antithesis between the people who 'turn' justice and righteousness into bitter refuse and the majestic creator who 'turns' darkness into morning and day into night (verse 8). He is the one of incomparable majesty. History is under his control. All are dependent on him. All are subject to his power.

Human perversion threatens to destroy the very means of sustaining life on earth, while God is constantly renewing his creation. He is in control, his power is unlimited. He made the constellations (Pleiades and Orion). Israel's favourite hymns positively affirmed his almighty power.

How could any person singing this hymn arrogantly tamper with God's purposes for creation through injustice and unrighteousness and think themselves immune from his awesome judgment? They are dealing with the Lord, not some Canaanite deity (like El and Baal) who were supposed to affect human destiny by influencing heavenly bodies.

God has power to create and also destroy (verse 9). He can execute swift judgment on the powerful in their fortresses (see also chapter 1, verse 2; chapter 3, verses 11, 12 and 15; chapter 4, verses 1 to 3). No defence system ('fortified city') can withstand his fury.

As Walter Wink writes:

> This myth [that people can defend themselves] speaks *for* God; it does not listen for God to speak. It invokes the sovereignty of God as its own; it does not entertain the prophetic possibility of radical denunciation and negation by God. It misappropriates the language, symbols and scriptures of Christianity. It does not seek God in order to change; it claims God in order to

prevent change.

> Its God is not the impartial ruler of all nations, but a biased and partial tribal god worshipped as an idol. Its metaphor is not the journey, but a fortress. Its symbol is not the cross, but a rod of iron. Its offer is not forgiveness, but victory. Its good news is not the unconditional love of enemies, but their final liquidation. Its salvation is not a new heart, but a successful foreign policy. It usurps the revelation of God's purposes for humanity in Jesus.
>
> It is blasphemous. It is idolatrous. And it is immensely popular.'[7]

Again a hymn of praise becomes an awesome invocation to God to be true to his character of righteousness and justice.

Worship calls his people to renew their covenant relationship so righteousness and justice can flow. If this doesn't happen, worship is sinful, says Amos.

God's case against the Israelites (verses 10 to 13)

This section expands on the general accusations of the rejection of righteousness and justice in chapter 5, verse 7.

Verse 10 is a frontal attack (using 'you') on those who deliberately controlled and manipulated the legal system to favour their interests. The wealthy and powerful through intimidation, bribes (verse 12) and pulling social strings demonstrated that they despised justice. They abhorred those who witnessed truthfully (verse 10) and made only a token effort to maintain the welfare of the people — by adhering to the letter of the law, rather than exhibiting a spirit of generosity.

In verses 11 and 12a, Amos hones in on economic exploitation. He directly accuses the unjust of harshly extorting (the Hebrew word translated 'trample' is a technical term for 'receive rent from') too much gain from the poor as rent for land — and probably also defrauding from them. Charging interest to the poor was forbidden by the Law, but the wealthy ignored God's call to treat such with compassion and return their lands in the Year of Jubilee (Leviticus 25).

The riches gained by injustice were not to be sustained. They would not enjoy their expensively built homes ('houses of. . . stone', verse 11, like those in the temple or king's palace — see also chapter 3, verse 15 and chapter 6, verse 4). The extensive vineyards planted on fields defrauded from the landless would provide them with no wine. Their ill-gotten luxuries were not signs of God's blessings as they presumed. They were signs of their continuous exploitation of the poor ('many offences', 'great sins': verse 12a).

God knew the facts. His curse, not his blessing would be on them. They harassed the innocent, stripped them of their rights and bought off the judges to get a favourable decision ('bribes'). As a result, the legal system was always stacked against the poor. This was injustice — exactly the opposite of God's commands to protect the poor (Deuteronomy 10, verse 18; Psalm 146, verse 9).

'Therefore' (verse 13) — the listener would surely expect a stern judgment statement, but in fact Amos leads into a type of proverb. The prophet is always throwing his readers off guard. In the sure day of judgment ('such times') with its complete destruction ('evil'), the oppressors would be silenced by God to accept their fate. Those who have suppressed the truth and drowned the cries of the oppressed will themselves be 'silenced by the inevitability of their own punishment'.[8]

It has been said that the most meaningful thing Western Christians can do is to be silent. If we stopped parading our schemes and solutions worldwide, we might be startled at what God has to say to us!

A plea from Amos (verses 14 and 15)
God's plea (in verses 4 to 7) to seek him came from the temple. This parallel plea to 'seek God' came from the courts. Here 'good' replaces 'Yahweh' in the seeking. Verses 14 and 15 follow (as in verse 4) the form of the priestly word, both with conditional promises of Yahweh's presence and mercy. These promises elaborate what Yahweh meant by 'live' (in

verse 4), the result of seeking him.

The starkness of parallelling opposites such as 'good/evil' (verse 14) and 'hate/love' (verse 15) is a form from wisdom literature, demonstrating not only powerfully opposing emotions, but the stark realities of Israel's choice — 'for' or 'against' Yahweh. Hating evil and doing justice is the only way to live and escape judgment.

Amos still hoped a few would respond to the challenge. The presence and protection of Yahweh, the God of hosts, could not be assumed as they claimed. Economic success, military might — even international security — were not indicators of God's presence. Even their election did not guarantee God's continuing favour (chapter 3, verses 1 and 2). 'Yahweh is with us' (verse 14b) was not a weapon for immunity (chapter 6, verse 3; chapter 9, verse 10). Their future was entirely conditional on restoring their relationship with Yahweh, not on their dogmas. The choice was theirs.

Effort was required — 'seek (verse 14), hate, love, maintain' (verse 15). Only deliberate choices and a determined reorientation of life to loving good and maintaining justice in the courts could lead to life instead of death.

To Amos, it was impossible to seek good by turning to Yahweh in religious activity unless the people also restored relations with one another. Good is shown in righteousness in social relationships, protected then by justice in the courts. This is the social order God designed. God's future kindness could not be guaranteed ('perhaps': verse 15), because he is not to be manipulated by any attempt at phony repentance. The Lord himself decides to whom he will show his kindness (Exodus 33, verse 19).

The plea, here, is not to hedge your bets or wring favour out of your history, but to change radically and to bow humbly before God in repentance. This is choosing life. Good must be demonstrated in daily relationships and in the insistence on justice.

Amos was realistic. Only a few would respond ('the remnant'). Most would be judged. They would choose death and continue in their egocentric rituals, economic exploitation, legal manipulations — deliberately pursuing evil and not good, thus choosing death, not life. But for some there was still hope.

A further obituary to Israel (verses 16 and 17)

Amos returns here to the lament of verses 1 to 3. Some listeners probably heard only the offer of hope. Amos was calling the people to avoid massive destruction through a radical reorientation of life. The people only indulged in cosmetic touches to get God on side. It was obvious. They were to ignore the prophet. Ahead there was only widespread grief — in the streets, public squares.

Landless farmers, a class non-existent before the eighth century, would bury their oppressors in their stolen land. The hollow grief of professional mourners is cold comfort for those who have abandoned mercy. Vineyards (verse 17) should have been places of rejoicing, but they were to be places of devastation — awful jibes here at wine they had so freely consumed at the expense of others (chapter 4, verse 1; chapter 5, verse 11b).

The cause of the devastation was God himself. The method of the 'passing through' (verse 17) is not stated. It may have taken the form of military invasion (chapter 5, verse 3; chapter 6, verse 14). But it was God, the Lord of hosts whom the people had to confront.

'I will pass through' (verse 17b) has overtones of God's protecting them from devastating plagues against Egypt (Exodus 11, verse 4; chapter 12, verse 12). But in this passage, God was not acting against a foreign heathen power, but against his own people. They had desecrated his majesty in self-centred worship. They had stripped the poor of their covenant rights to justice and righteousness. They had belittled all Yahweh's attempts to restore precious relationships.

When God's hand of death was to fall, their grief would be like that of the Egyptians. Yahweh would surely come to those who would not seek him.

Discussion questions

Talking it through

1 What sorts of 'human' qualities does this passage reveal that God has? How does this make you feel? Does it increase or decrease your confidence in God?

2 In verses 8 and 9, praise is seen to be ineffectual if our attitude is not right. We may not have a 'fortress' (verse 9) in the same sense, but how can our attitudes be fortress-like? How can this impede our worship?

3 What is justice? At which points in this passage was justice not exercised? Why is this such a concern to God?

Widening our horizons

1 Where should the course of justice lie in each of the following situations?
  (a) The right of an individual not to pay taxes to his/her government
  (b) The right of the individual to bear arms
  (c) The right of the individual to engage in commercial activity without any legal constraints
  (d) The right to get a financial return on one's investment or capital asset.
  Are all of equal 'weight'? Examine each in some detail, then come up with a general statement of what constitutes 'justice' that takes into account these various issues.

2 What does it mean to be 'vulnerable to God'? What barriers do we erect that make us *less* vulnerable to God? Consider:
  (a) Inequity between the Third and First Worlds
  (b) Care for aged and disabled relatives
  (c) Possessions we want, but don't need
  (d) Workaholism and frenetic activity.

3 Does this chapter of Amos shed any different light on Matthew 7, verse 21 for you?

> Not everyone who says to me, 'Lord, Lord,' will enter the kingdom of heaven, but only he who does the will of my Father who is in heaven (NIV).

4 McAfee Brown writes:

> If we[in the US] asked our friends in the Third World to tell us what gods they perceive us worshipping, really worshipping, no matter what we say our ultimate loyalties are, the list might look something like this:
>
> Keeping the United States No. 1 at all costs
>
> Maintaining absolute superiority over any other nation in guns, tanks, nuclear weapons
>
> The right to decide who should govern countries that might otherwise 'threaten' us
>
> The right to have a 'good life' even at the expense of other people or nations
>
> Operating within an economic system that nobody tries to regulate

We may not find such a list flattering to our egos, individual or national, but in our more candid moments we can sometimes admit that such are, indeed, operative 'gods' for many within our culture.

And at that point, for those who feel some uneasiness in worshipping such deities, the question is posed: When the power of such gods is so great

in our land, how can we risk affirming the God of
Shadrach, Meshach and Abednego, of Abraham,
Sarah, Jesus, the Jews, Archbishop Romero? Such
an act of faith seems a very long shot: no
assurances, no guarantees — and even the odds
aren't particularly appealing (sometimes six million
to none). Such a God can save us from the power
of the other gods, but then again, such a God might
not. . .

A struggle with that dilemma will characterise
the rest of our lives, if we are serious about it.[9]

(a) To what extent is this accurate for your
culture. . . your community. . . your
family?

(b) How do you respond to the risk of
affirming the authority in your life of
the God of Amos?

6
Relationships based on false hopes

AMOS CHAPTER 5, VERSE 18 TO CHAPTER 6, VERSE 14

IN THIS PASSAGE, AMOS DELIVERS two 'woe oracles': the first at chapter 5, verse 18 and the second at chapter 6, verse 1, each of them against the false hopes and securities which were preventing Israel from renewing its relationship with Yahweh. These delusions were fed by their theological conservatism and ill-gotten affluence. Both oracles mourn the end with a prediction, the first one of exile (chapter 5, verse 27) and the second one of invasion (chapter 6, verse 14). Woe oracles are like funeral laments, with the grieving sobs of loss and devastation moving towards the desire for revenge.

The prophet had just read the obituary of the nation: evil was triumphing over good (chapter 5, verses 14 and 15); the upper class showed no righteousness or justice to the poor (chapter 5, verses 7, 10 to 13). Yahweh had to respond: armies were destroyed (chapter 5, verse 3), the wealthy were made homeless (chapter 5, verse 11) and there was wailing everywhere (chapter 5, verse 16 and 17).

The message was impossible to believe. Surely wealth, national peace, a flourishing religious system and international prestige indicated that God was with them? Surely they as a people of God were to be vindicated on that day when Yahweh would assert his authority over all the earth?

They had reached the point where their religion had become the enemy of justice and righteousness and thus of reality. In the midst of all these dire warnings, Amos still had hope that Israel might respond. He continued to plead (chapter 5, verses 23 and 24).

Israel had no future (chapter 5, verses 18 to 27)

Amos focusses his argument first on a cherished hope clear to his hearers — 'the day of the Lord' (verse 18). This concept was central to Israel's theology. Here is its earliest Old Testament reference. The people knew it well.

'The day of the Lord' was anticipated as the great

victory of Yahweh over all worlds seen and unseen. As his elect people, Israel would have the glorious role as victorious nation. All enemies would fall beneath her feet.

Amos may have been speaking at the celebrations at the Bethel shrine: rousing singing, luxurious feasting, excessive sacrificing (chapter 4, verse 4f; chapter 5, verse 21ff) — all accompanied by the fervent affirmation, 'Yahweh is with us' (chapter 5, verse 14b). This was a convenient theology for a people who saw themselves as carving out an illustrious destiny among the surrounding inferior nations. What was shocking was the prophet's association of this day with a cry of woe, a funeral lament with its ominous sound of desperation — not the note of joy, they expected.

Again here (as in chapter 3, verse 2 and chapter 9, verse 7), Amos takes up a popular aspect of the people's theology and uses it against them. The theology of 'the day of the Lord' needed no re-visiting, but its relational base did. The day offered no security apart from a restoration of covenant relationships between Yahweh and his people.

Theology is never a substitute for intimacy. Divorced from relationships, theology becomes ideology — a weapon for perverted aspirations, ultimately for unreality. It was Amos' own encounters with Yahweh (in his visions in chapter 7, verses 1 to 9 and chapter 8, verses 1 to 3) which gave these interpretations of theology such startling urgency and certainty. 'The day of the Lord' would bring judgment, not victory.

❑ *There was no future for the people (verses 18 to 20).*

'Why are you so hopeful?', asked Amos. In effect he said in verses 18 to 20, 'Do you realise that your passionate longings will deliver the very reversal of what you hoped — darkness, not light; danger and fear, not security and freedom?' Israel anticipated this for her enemies, not for herself.

Two parables drawn from country life make his point clear (verse 19). Just when you think you are secure, there is unexpected danger. Fleeing from a lion, you meet a bear. Then safe inside your home, you are bitten by a snake.

These homely parables stress Amos' original point. There will only be darkness, not light — pitch black darkness. Be realistic, said Amos (verse 20). Yahweh will wage war against his enemies. But his enemies are his chosen people, Israel.

❑ *There was no future for the religious cult (verses 21 to 24).*

The religious cult, zealous and extravagant, perpetuated the delusions of a bright future. It was totally condemned (verses 21 to 24). 'I hate. . . despise,' God said (verse 21).

Total, nauseous disgust can be expressed no more strongly. 'I cannot stand' (verse 21b) literally means, 'I do not inhale with delight', vividly conveying God's absolute revulsion at such abuse of worship. He disassociated himself from all their cultic activity: 'your feasts', 'your assemblies'. His first person language is fierce and biting, displaying the intensity of loathing and a rejection that must take action: 'I will not accept them', 'I will have no regard for them' (verse 22).

Every essential aspect of the nation's worship was condemned: feasts and assemblies at the annual pilgrim festivals (including Passover and Unleavened Bread, Harvest and Booths), burnt offerings, grain offerings and 'offerings of well-being' (verse 22).

None was to be accepted. In fact, their worship was an act of sin, as Amos suggested earlier (chapter 4, verses 4 and 5). God found their hollow music particularly annoying and called urgently for it to stop (verse 23). 'No more,' denounced Yahweh. How different it was when Yahweh encouraged people to worship (Psalm 33, verses 2 and 3). Why had it now become so obnoxious?

The reason for God's vehement 'No!' is in verse 24. The form is one of instruction, but the message is one of judgment. Worship is useless unless it is associated with unstinting ('waters') and unceasing ('everflowing') acts of righteousness and justice.

Doing justice is central to true worship. Righteous living is a prerequisite of worship. All relationships must bear the marks of consistency with these covenant standards, especially to the poor and weak. Otherwise worshippers cannot expect God's approval. The worshipping community must also live as God's community (Matthew 7, verse 21).

God wants a mighty river of justice, similar to that which flowed from the hillsides after a sudden thunderstorm. A temporary wadi (or billabong) is not sufficient. Those who truly love and worship God are marked by a constant concern for the rights and welfare of all his people. The shrines of Bethel, Gilgal and Beersheba encouraged merely noisy activity — words, not deeds. Without deeds, words were distasteful and useless. Lives of righteousness and deeds of justice could only flow out of a renewed relationship with Yahweh. This cult was preventing that renewal. The covenant had been corrupted into selfish, racist, 'insurance' religion.

Amos was not arguing here for non-cultic versus cultic (non-formal versus formal) religion . But this particular cult was sinful and useless. It propped up vested interests and fed national pride. The signs of the community of God in action — justice and righteousness (chapter 6, verse 12; chapter 5, verses 7 and 15) — were absent. So Amos called them to abandon the religious systems and start acting righteously to their neighbours and ensure justice for all, particularly the weak. At the basis of this travesty were broken relationships.

❑ *There was no future in disobedience, history had shown (verses 26 and 27).*

Amos now faced the people with more reality to further unearth the roots of their deceptive religiosity (verses 25 and 27). Yahweh first (verse 25) called his people to reflect on a section of their cherished salvation history.

'Even in the wilderness,' Yahweh asked, 'did our relationship depend on the cult (sacrifices) and offerings alone?' Of course, the answer is 'no'. There, the people had to also act in righteousness and justice. Worship, then, came from hearts of faith and love. The past is idealised to set in stark relief Israel's sinfulness through current cultic extravagence. To Amos, the exodus, wilderness and conquest of the land and covenant demonstrated the relationships God wanted with his chosen people.

The second accusing statement in verse 26 is difficult. The sense is: 'You carried (now carry or will carry) around images of your king and your star god that you made for yourself.' The reference may be to idolatrous influences from the Tigris-Euphrates Valley — some astral deities, venerated as kings, whom Israel would be forced to worship in exile. Amos was accusing the people of not responding to Yahweh out of repentant, loving hearts and faithful obedience – they should, instead, have been emulating their forefathers' faithfulness in the wilderness (chapter 5, verse 25). Rather, they chose (or were forced to choose) to include idols in their cultic rituals (chapter 8, verse 14). Coupled with consistent ruthlessness and injustice, God had no choice but to send them into exile (verse 27).

The God of hosts had put his seal on this horrific decision. Exile meant displacement from the very place where they and their fathers had experienced Yahweh's covenant promises. From bondage in Egypt to freedom in the land, they chose bondage again. Records verify that the Assyrians did later exile Israel 'beyond Damascus' (2 Kings 17, verses 23 and 24). But to Amos, Yahweh himself exiled his people.

Israel had no security (chapter 6, verses 1 to 14)

Amos was in the process of unmasking the unreality of the people's deceptive expectations, particularly about their future (chapter 5, verses 18 to 27) and their security (chapter 6, verses 1 to 14). The powerful were not seeking God or justice (chapter 5, verses 4 to 6, 14 and 15). They flaunted their oppression of the poor by building ostentatious homes (chapter 5, verses 10 to 13). Death and destruction were inevitable (chapter 5, verses 16 and 17).

But the people continued to have false hopes of

being on the winning side on the 'day of the Lord' (chapter 5, verse 18). They had diligently performed more than the required number of rituals (chapter 5, verses 21 to 23). But God said they had no future. Amos attempted to pull down their false hopes about an even more brilliant future.

They had presumed their nation would be secure for ever and bolstered themselves with a theology to prove it. Theology at the service of heartless complacency is a terrifying tyrant. For Dietrich Bonhoeffer, a church that prizes fidelity to the aims of the nation above the demands of the gospel was a church enchained to an idol.[1]

Obviously, the outburst against the religious systems of chapter 5 had little effect. Excessive religious enthusiasm must surely please God and keep him on side – why else would their nation be so powerful, the economy so booming, their usual enemies so weak? Nothing less seemed like a disaster. There was no seeking of renewed life in God (chapter 5, verse 5).

Amos' next oracle is about their false sense of security (chapter 6, verses 1 to 14). He focusses on their ruthless complacency (verses 1 to 7), pride (verses 8 to 11) and strength (verses 12 to 14).

❑ *There was to be no security for the complacent (verses 1 to 7).*

You think you are flourishing in your carefree luxury (verse 1)? asks Amos. The two nations, Israel and

Judah, bear the full force of God's fury. Jerusalem ('Zion') is included with Samaria. The rich and the prestigious again are the focus of the prophet's blast. The undercurrent is full of irony.

Their ease ('complacent': verse 1) is irresponsible; their confidence ill-founded. Encouraging others to fawn over them for guidance and advice was hypocritical. Amos scathingly challenged their stance of personal ('notable') and national ('foremost') superiority (verse 2). These nations were under judgment. What was their advice worth? Their only destiny was to be the head ('first': verse 7) of the exiles.

Amos' listeners delivered an angry, well-documented rebuttal of this statement of doom (verse 2). The prophet often used his contenders' quotations as evidence against them (verse 13, for example). Compared with a wide survey of the neighbours (Calnesh and Hamath were northern city states; Gath was a city west of Jerusalem), Israel and Judah were impregnable, expansive and affluent — truly, superior.

The exact location of these places is uncertain, but it is clear that all three were former city states whose glories were receding in the constant power ferment of the Near East. This seeming compliment to national pride becomes a weapon of judgment. How can the futures of Israel and Judah be any different from these cities?

Amos marshalled all his brilliant verbal sarcasm

as he castigated the people face-to-face (verse 3). What they should have faced up to (the judgment of 'the day of the Lord': chapter 5, verses 18 to 20; chapter 8, verse 10), they actually 'put far away' ('exclude from fellowship' in Hebrew), ignoring its fateful consequences. On the other hand, the violence, oppression and exploitation that they should not have allowed to have any control over them, they actually invited to have an intimate role in their lives.

Then comes an ugly picture of a sham feast (verses 4 to 6), probably from a funeral ceremony meant to honour the dead and comfort the mourning (as in Jeremiah 16, verses 4 to 9). The whole ceremony has become a pathetic travesty given to selfish indulgence and celebrating (not mourning) the 'ruin of Joseph', the ruin of their nation (verse 6). The people sprawled immodestly on their ivory beds, greedily feasting.

Ivory (verse 4) was the sign of royal opulence and also of exploiting of the poor in foreign conquests. *Lounge* (verse 4) implies the carefree, undisciplined indulgence of those who carelessly flaunt their excessive lifestyles to others. *Lambs* (a meal for the wealthy: verse 4), carefully chosen and specially fattened on grain stolen from the poor (chapter 5, verse 11), demonstrated inexcusable inequality and waste to Amos. Meat was eaten by the poor only at celebrations (Luke 15, verse 23) or peace offerings (chapter 5, verse 22).

Relationships based on false hopes/137

In their crudely improvised drunken ballads (verse 5), they liked to consider themselves equal to David with his great musical ability. But he played for the glory of God and to celebrate real victories. The tragic scene here is of the perversion of creativity for the purpose of drunken orgies. Drinking wine by the bowlfuls and massaging themselves with the most extravagant oils (verse 6), they were oblivious to the impending death of their nation. The covenant name 'Joseph' for Israel here adds special pathos.

Amos announced certain judgment with an ironic twist on the word 'first' (verse 7) after his use of 'first' in verse 1. The so-called first people were the first *exiles* — those to go way beyond Damascus (chapter 5, verse 27). When the Babylonians later invaded Jerusalem (2 Kings 24, verses 14 to 16), they particularly seized the leaders and the skilled. Samaria was never again independent, nor did any of its descendants rule as king over the nation.

Their arrogant complacency and life of ruthless leisure at the expense of the poor would all come to an end, says Amos. Then, there would be a true funeral, not a mockery.

❏ *There was to be no security for the proud (verses 8 to 11).*
The threat of judgment now became the irrevocable word of Yahweh, the God of hosts. He also was the

divine warrior, the One sovereign over all the heavenly armies as well as those on earth who enact his commands. The repetition of his name (verse 8) stressed his total commitment to his decision. The phrase 'by himself' (meaning 'by his life' or, literally, 'by his throat') indicates that no higher power can be invoked. God stakes his very character and integrity on this solemn decision (as in chapter 4, verse 2 and chapter 8, verse 7).

The strongest possible language is used to express God's response to sinful arrogance ('abhor', 'detest': verse 8). His majesty should have been the focus of the people's trust, not their own preening wilfulness. The nation is called Jacob here again, a fitting symbol of self-manipulated glory. God detested the way the urban 'fortresses' had become the centres of luxury, violence, deceptive national hopes and presumed invulnerability. Humility and trust needed to be the centre of relationships. God would personally and thoroughly supervise the destruction of pride, which was in fact idolatry and totally abhorrent (Deuteronomy 7, verses 25 and 26).

The coming devastation was to be complete (verse 9). Those left would only face death. A possible plague associated with invasion might be so extensive that bodies, usually buried, would have to be burnt (verse 10). Cremation was not the usual practice among Israelites. Those searching for the bodies of plague victims would silence any attempt to pray for God's mercy. Even to call on his name ('hush' has a cultic overtone as a call to silence before Yahweh) might have invited more devastation. The language is abrupt, reflecting the coldness of shock and disbelief. Yahweh would do this to his chosen people. It is frightening to be in the hands of the Lord of hosts.

Like a ruthless military commander, he would take command of the destruction (verse 11) as he said he would (verse 8). Total destruction (for 'great house' and 'small house') was the result, maybe by means of an earthquake, which in other parts of Amos indicated God's direct activity (chapter 1, verse 1; chapter 2, verse 13; chapter 8, verse 8; chapter 9, verses 1 to 6).

This is the powerful wrath of God, which challenges all human pride. The nation was to become one large pile of rubble.

❏ *There was to be no security for the strong (verses 12 to 14).*

Then the prophet surprises with a change of pace and tone using his masterful rhetorical questions again to highlight the incredible nature of Israel's rebellion.

Only a madman would try to run horses on rocky cliffs (verse 12a)! How absurd to plough the sea with oxen (verse 12b)! These silly questions may have even brought a smile to the readers after such heavy invective. But the absurd had become the astonishing reality in Israel. The people had perverted justice into poison and the effects of righteousness into bitterness (compare chapter 5, verses 7 and 24).

To Amos, Israel's identity was established by covenant relationships — with Yahweh and with one another. Righteousness was the quality of life expected of all those in covenant relationship. Justice guarded these relationships through the courts. Relying on the integrity of the participant, justice was the 'fruit of righteousness' (verse 12). However, where the poor expected their rights to be honoured by the justice of the courts, they were treated unjustly (chapter 5, verses 10 to 15).

This was a ruthless perversion of covenant relations with Yahweh and with other so-called people of God. Equally absurd was their pollution of worship (chapter 5, verses 21 to 24). Absurd, but horrifyingly true.

How equally illogical it was to trust in short-lived military might (verse 13), especially when the name of one of the towns defeated, Lo Debar, means 'nothing' (a pun by the author).

Amos enjoyed ironic plays on words and meanings. The other town, 'Karnaim' (translated in the NIV as 'horns'), means 'might', indicating the people's vain boast that the victory had been by their own impressive strength. But the singing and dancing are hollow. They have had victory over nothing.

No-one has victory unless Yahweh gives it. He is the divine warrior in charge of all the movements of peoples of the earth. The actual situation (outlined in general terms in Amos 1, verses 3 to 5) probably reflected the capture of these Syrian towns first by Jeroboam II and then by Assyria. But here the people of God were claiming to be able to command the movements of people in war. Their boasting was not only absurd: it was detestable and dangerous. God's power would not be usurped; he would show who was in charge of history (chapter 9, verse 7).

The sure word of the Lord (verse 14: an elaboration on verse 11) was that another nation would be chosen and blessed with victory over Israel. The nation was not named, but hinted at in chapter 5, verse 27 ('beyond Damascus'). This nation would not muster up its own military might, but God would raise it up. The devastation would be complete: from the northernmost limits (Lebo-hamath) to its southern most limits to the Dead Sea (also called Wadi Arabah) — the full extent of the grandeur of Solomon and Jeroboam's reign.

This was to be the awful result for those who did not trust their God as their source of hope about the future and security. The deception of the strong wielding power over the weak to bolster their own ease, security and opulence was exposed in all its despicable corruption. The future was not the stage for the ruthless manipulation of military, economic or even religious powers. Without God as the true stronghold, the raw forces of greed and oppression make everything that is sweet and merciful in life, bitter and death-producing (verse 12b).

Discussion questions

Talking it through

1 Why do you think God's reaction to the worship and offerings in verses 21 and 22 is so strong? Verse 24 should provide a starting point to the answer.

Is it an appropriate response by God, do you think? Does this quote help you?

Righteousness and justice are not abstract levels of legality. They are terms of relationship.

2 What criteria were the people using to make a judgment about whether God was pleased with them or not? Why is that an unreliable guide?

3 God's condemnation of the Israelites was not simply that they lived in luxury (verses 4 to 7); it was something more. What else was it?

What clues are there in verses 4 to 7 that this is so? Is there any reason to think

144/Relationships based on false hopes

that such criticism could not be levelled at people who live in luxury today?

4 What indications are there in verses 9 to 14 that the destruction of Israel was to be complete? Why does God act so comprehensively?

What point is being made that has application to us?

Widening our horizons

1 Dietrich Bonhoeffer has said:

> Our being a Christian today is limited by two things: prayer and doing justice amongst men.

How true is this of Christians today?

2 Read this story about Pastor Joseph:

> Late Friday afternoon, they stormed the squatters' homes. Ten huge trucks to cart away scrap iron and timber that have been people's homes for twenty years. Fifteen armed guards with machine guns threatening distressed families, just cooking their evening rice. Demolition raids always occur at this time. The people are most vulnerable, tired and cut off from any legal redress over the weekend.
> Protesters were arrested on 1000 peso bail — an impossible amount. It is expensive, let alone dangerous, to stand up for justice. Pastor Joseph bundled his people into a school. Churches were burnt. He would not leave them. He would fight for justice.[2]

How does this account give flesh to the notion that justice must be expressed by purposeful action, not just talked about?

3 'Any system which takes success as its criterion denies the crucifixion.' Do you believe this to be true? What does this tell you about:
(a) God?
(b) the Christian lifestyle?

4 Consider the following statement: 'Theology is never a substitute for intimacy. Divorced from relationships, theology becomes ideology — a weapon for perverted aspirations, ultimately for unreality' (page 125).

(a) Is this really true? What examples have you seen in the church where a loveless Christianity has led to alienation and self-delusion? How can we keep our theological ideals tied into our personal relationships?
(b) How helpful is theology to developing intimacy with God? Do we need a new kind of theology? How could it encourage intimacy with God?
(c) What is the danger of any ideology? Why can it easily become dogma or demonic? What are some safeguards to keep the winds of the Spirit blowing through our fondest theological beliefs?

7
The consequences of fractured relationships

AMOS CHAPTER 7, VERSE 1 TO
CHAPTER 9, VERSE 10

A NEW DIRECTION COMES IN AMOS at this point. Five visions become a living drama of God's intentions for his people (chapter 7, verses 1 to 8; chapter 8, verses 1 and 2; chapter 9, verses 1 to 6). Amos had personal and authoritative evidence from the sovereign Lord himself. His perceptions become even clearer of God's judgment of Israel's deluded assumptions and false hopes (chapter 3, verse 1 to chapter 6, verse 14). Now comes the fulfilment, powerfully enacted before the prophet (chapter 7, verse 1 to chapter 9, verse 10).

The visions set out the terrifying stages of God's

inevitable response to his people who had so abused their relationships. Amos took up their cherished tenents of national piety and reaffirmed their original significance — a loving commitment to Yahweh and one another that involves covenanted relationships. We encounter here an overwhelming urgency, an increasing compulsion and an authority to the prophetic message.

All the visions display the intimacy of face-to-face encounters with Yahweh. Amos struggles to deal with God's mysterious sovereignty. He knows God so he dares to question, plead and accuse God of neglecting his covenant responsibilities. He intercedes and calls God to mediate with desperate urgency. The focus, though, is always on Yahweh who relentlessly plunges the prophet into vision after vision of judgment (chapter 7, verses 8 and 15; chapter 8, verse 2), yet never without reminders of his mercy. But the trading on God's kindness would inevitably come to an end.

These visions represent no private spiritual titillations to get a few pictures from God. This is a consuming, indeed involuntary encounter with Yahweh (literally 'my master Yahweh': chapter 7, verses 1 and 2, 4 to 6; chapter 8, verses 1, 3, 9 and 11). Four of the five visions — the exception is chapter 8, verses 1 and 2 — highlight this awesome presence of Yahweh.

Amos is not a free agent to listen casually and

attempt personal surmises of interpretation. He has been snatched out of his profession and plunged into an alien urban world of another nation, with no choice but to speak out the terrifying power of God's words. His bitter encounter with the cultic priest Amaziah (chapter 7, verses 10 to 17) fits between visions three and four to starkly contrast the one who was consumed with the Almighty sovereign over all time and the one who was at the mercy of conniving confusions of his own times.

Yahweh is master (chapter 9, verse 24), therefore everything (every people, system, force) must submit to his authority. The alternative would be terrifying devastation. How much warning do the people need?

VISION 1: Locusts (chapter 7, verses 1 to 3

This vision is not just a daydream for Amos. God himself showed Amos how he prepared the plague (verse 1). Locusts were dreaded not only for their devastating effects of despair and famine, but also for their representation as the wrath of Yahweh against Israel.

The timing of this plague suggests that the king and his court provided well for themselves from taxes on the first harvest crop. If the locusts stripped the second crop, the small farmers and peasants would be left with nothing. The authoritative source of the vision — Yahweh himself — ensured the certain repetition of the dream in real life. Amos saw it as if it were happening. Obviously, he assumed that the sins of the previous chapters (1 to 6) caused the plague. There was no sign of repentance. If God forgave, it would only be because of his grace.

As mediator, the prophet marshalled no covenant promise, as Israel's election had become the basis for judgment, not immunity. There is a tender element to the covenant in calling Israel 'Jacob'. This was Amos' favourite name for the northern kingdom (chapter 3, verse 13; chapter 6, verse 8; chapter 8, verse 7; chapter 9, verse 8), identifying it here with Jacob the lesser one whom God chose and was obligated to help in his weakness. But Israel was parading self-congratulatory invulnerability (chapter 6, verses 1ff, 8 and 13). The prophet unmasked the unreality of their self-sufficiency. He pleads for forgiveness for them as a helpless, insignificant nation ('so small': verse 2).

This was the truth about Israel: they were small, weak and vulnerable, whatever unrealistic grandiose views they had of themselves. 'The unmasking of illusion belongs to the essence of the contemplative life,' says Thomas Merton, who exposes the danger of false spirituality in modern life.[1] But Yahweh is passionately concerned for the weak and poor (chapter 2, verses 6 to 8). The people's survival depended on their *accepting* this humbling reversal of their cherished boasts and their attempts at justifying the exploiting of the poor. But, as yet, they had no change of heart. There was no denouncing of the powers of domination. It was *Yahweh* who changed ('relented': verse 3).

He responded with compassion for this poor nation on the verge of extinction. Being always free to 'relent' or change is in keeping with his character of love (see Genesis 6, verse 6; Joel 2, verses 13 and 14). Yahweh willingly and warmly withholds his judgment because of the prophet Amos' pleading.

How much more he would have done if the people had repented. The circumstances provoking the locusts' judgment remain unchanged.

VISION 2: Fire (chapter 7, verses 4 to 6)

Fire, too, is God's agent of judgment in Amos' second vision. Its enormous power dried up the subterranean water and destroyed the land, a precious gift from Yahweh. 'The great deep' (verse 4) may have been a jibe by Amos at the power of God to completely overwhelm some eastern pagan religions which deified the deep.

Judgment by fire is common in Amos against those who usurp God's sovereignty.[2] This time the prophet only begged God to stop. Repentance did not seem possible. Again the plea was on the basis of the people's vulnerability: 'How can Jacob survive? He is so small' (verse 5a).

God was gracious again. Yet the overtone is clear at what would happen if his grace were removed.

How strategic is the role of the intercessor, standing as intermediary between God's judgment and the people. 'History belongs to the intercessors', says Wink, 'who spiritually defy what is, in the name of what God has promised.'[3]

VISION 3: Plumbline (chapter 7, verses 7 and 8)

This vision from God is of an ordinary plumbline. Amos could identify it, but its purpose was a mystery. The prophet was actively involved in the awesome dialogue with Yahweh who explained he was using the plumbline to test the true standing of his people. The vision established not just the fact of judgment (as the first two visions), but its necessity. Amos did not even intercede.

Used for the first time, 'my people Israel' (verse 8) refers to the personal covenant relationship between God and Israel outlined in chapter 3, verse 2 (cf. Exodus 3, verse 10 and Deuteronomy 4, verse 20).[4] This is the measure for the people's character and faithfulness. So the judgment announced is agonising for God. He is in loving relationship with these people, but his longsuffering must end. There will be more pleading from Amos. His insights into election theology in chapter 3, verse 2 are painfully clarified: there will be judgment, not blessing and certainly no immunity.

The two main national institutions were doomed for destruction: the religious shrines ('high places of Isaac' and 'sanctuaries of Israel': verse 9) and the royal court ('house of Jeroboam'). The people were to be cut off from the great fathers of the covenant Isaac and Jacob (Israel). The popular tradition of worshipping at the northern shrines of Bethel (verse 13) and Dan or at the shrine to honour Isaac's birthplace of Beersheba (chapter 5, verse 5 and chapter 8, verse 14) were to cease.

Verse 10 of 2 Kings 15 records the destruction of Jeroboam II's dynasty. Yahweh himself was the executioner of his own people. It was unthinkable. Yahweh would use the sword (verse 9b).

Amos and Amaziah (chapter 7, verses 10 to 17)

Now comes an abrupt break from the visions. Amos and the false prophet Amaziah clash violently. Amos wins, not through force of argument or superior tricks, but through his dependence on Yahweh as the source of all he says, sees and does.

Amaziah charges Amos with plotting treason against King Jeroboam and his country (verse 11). Amaziah was probably high priest because of his high courtly access. The Bethel shrine, where Amaziah presided, was a sanctuary of the king — a state temple (verse 13).

The Bethel shrine followed the traditions of

Jeroboam I (1 Kings 12) who, after dividing from the southern kingdom, set up a religious cult to rival that of Jerusalem. It had golden calves, non-Levitical priests and new festivals, and became more an expression of fervent nationalism than of humble obedience to Yahweh.

As a political manoeuverer and pawn of the state, Amaziah perverts the words of Amos. Warnings of judgment (chapter 7, verse 9), critiques of the cult (chapter 5, verse 5) and predictions of exile (chapter 5, verse 27; chapter 6, verse 7) became fuel for Amaziah's paranoia about political intrigue and personal threat. The simmering, ugly hatred for his personal rival became unbearable. Sounding pious, Amaziah claimed, 'The land is not able to bear [contain] his words' (verse 10).

The picture here is of a bronze laver spilling over its contents (see 1 Kings 7, verses 26 and 38). Amos' powerful prophecy threatened to fill the land with calls for justice and righteousness — or judgment. While Amaziah was claiming religious legitimacy for the nation's political, economic and social ruthlessness, God's plumbline measured accurately the wide discrepancy between religious hypocrisy and his covenantal provisions.

Again Amos warned that God would use the sword in judgment (verse 11). It would kill Amaziah's own family (verse 17), prevent others fleeing from the collapsed sanctuary (chapter 9, verse 1)

— even hunt them down in exile (chapter 9, verse 4), and end all their lying complacency (chapter 9, verse 10). Exile is a common threat from Amos[5] and, despite Amaziah's vitriolic taunts, was to be also his inevitable destiny with his people in a pagan country (verse 17).

Amaziah spat out his vengeance against Amos and his message. Amaziah saw that his king (Jeroboam), his beloved nation and his prestigious role were all under threat. 'You're just a southern prophet' is in effect what Amaziah was saying (verse 12). With such a snide slur, Amaziah, bristling with authority, sought to ban Amos from prophesying at Bethel and order him home where his prophesying would be more socially acceptable and possibly lucrative ('earn your bread': verse 12). Expelling Amos meant stifling these announcements of death and destruction against the king and his temple.

But Amos' defence is clear. He was a prophet. He submitted to no authority other than that of Yahweh. His prophesying in Israel was a divine appointment, a position he didn't seek and for which, humanly speaking, he was untrained. He was not in a business venture as a member of a professional prophet band bolstering national pride and cursing enemies (chapter 2, verse 11 and chapter 3, verses 7 and 8). He was a shepherd, maybe a manager of other shepherds, and a farmer of sycamore and fig trees (verse 14). God caused the radical and surprising change in his life (verse 15).

His wide-ranging business interests allowed him to travel all over Judah and Israel and to learn first hand about the national crises. His long hours tending cattle and closeness to the soil kept his perceptions alert and untrammelled by fawning praise of superiors or the manipulation by powerful interests. In challenging the will of God in Amos, Amaziah was defying God himself. The call on Amos was irresistible (chapter 3, verses 7 and 8). God's word is all powerful, subordinating the words of every other man and consuming all lesser professions (verse 15).

Amos' reply was bare and terse. He claimed no divine visions here as substantiating evidence. There is no argument, only a frightening boldness as Amos delivered another word from God to the priest himself (verses 16 to 18). Amaziah was the one to be expelled, not Amos. The horrible future of his family involved: prostitution for his wife (probably to invaders to the city), murder for his children, loss of his property, a humiliating and ceremonially unclean death on heathen soil — as well as exile for his whole country. Amaziah, so proudly secure in his religious position, was to be stripped of all his qualifications and privileges: an honourable marriage, a continuing priestly line, land (possibly a gift from the king) and a dignified burial. Such was the devastation of the judgment of God for this false prophet and the people.

Amos continued to live and speak daringly to challenge those vested interests which seemed most capable of destroying him. No safe option in Judah for him. Obedience to the will of Yahweh was his only true safety. There was no personal defence or claim to authority. Yahweh's word had consumed him. An old tradition says Amaziah had Amos' teeth broken to silence him. No scepticism or opposition could quell the authentic call and word of God (chapter 2, verse 12 and chapter 3, verses 7 and 8). His authority to relay visions from God was reaffirmed.

VISION 4: Summer fruit
(chapter 8, verses 1 to 3)

This next vision is of a basket of ripe fruit, possibly an offering at the Bethel shrine by a worshipper hoping it would ensure security and prosperity for the future. The explanation is based on a play on words between 'summer fruit' and 'ripe'. The season has ended (the fruit is ripe).

The time has also ended for God's people. It will be devastating (verse 2). It was the end of God's covenant relationship. Forgiveness was no longer available. Mercy was exhausted (chapter 7, verse 8).

No longer would the Bethel temple be filled with optimism, misguided though it was. Joyful hymns would be replaced with wailing (chapter 5, verses 16 and 17). The many exposed corpses demonstrate the most shameful curse possible on the dead — to remain unburied.

'On that day' (verse 3), the day of Yahweh (chapter 2, verse 16; chapter 8, verses 9 and 13), he would still be victor, but his very own people would be his victims. The only response was stunned silence. Those who used worship to manipulate Yahweh for a better life would only find death.

Five signs of the end (chapter 8, verses 4 to 14)

Five short judgment speeches or oracles now flashed out the awful reality of the fourth vision (chapter 8, verses 1 to 3) that the end had come. Signs of the end multiply: merciless exploitation of the poor (verses 4 to 7); a terrifying earthquake (chapter 8, verse 8), a darkened sun (verses 9 and 10), the absence of God's word (verses 11 and 12), and dire thirst (verses 13 and 14).

All are stark signs of the withdrawal of God's favour. His covenant has been irreparably violated. Total terror is everywhere. There is absolute certainty of this.

❏ *The first sign of the end: the poor are exploited (verses 4 to 7)*

The listeners are required to consider this key feature of covenant violation. 'Hear this' (verse 4) is the common way for Amos to command attention.[6] Amos cleverly (verse 5), as before, quotes the listeners' words against them.[7] 'Let's get worship over so we can get back to business' is a paraphrase of what is being said in verse 5.

Impatient and hollow piety on holy days (new moon and sabbath: verse 5) masked an insatiable greed for money. In the changing of Israelite society into a money economy, a commercial class was emerging. The poor were ruthlessly trampled in the flush of the new wealth. It is always geared against them, especially by those who could manipulate the system (by means, for instance, of false weights, measures, scales: chapter 8, verse 5).

With a total disregard for the poor, traders cheated, extorted and enslaved them for minor debts. Progress should never mean trading neighbours as commercial commodities or selling refuse ('sweepings') for profit (verse 6). The picture is of people consumed by profit and deadened to the One who rescued them from the oppressors; they are called to treat the poor and needy in righteousness and justice. In the successful frenzy of both religious cults and markets, Yahweh was forgotten.

These covenant atrocities are indelibly scoured into Yahweh's memory. A busy cultic life was no substitute for justice (chapter 5, verse 24). This time, Yahweh's solemn oath was neither by his holiness (chapter 4, verse 2), nor by his own character (chapter 6, verse 8), but by his now sarcastic name — 'the pride of Jacob' (verse 7). Their actions hardly showed they were proud of Yahweh. They had denigrated his name, elevating their own ruthless pride (chapter 6, verse 8).

Yahweh's judgments would be enacted. There was no doubt that all were accountable.

❏ *The second sign of the end: a terrifying earthquake (chapter 8, verse 8)*

For all of this, could the people logically expect anything less than God's judgment? An earthquake is the common sign of this in Amos.[8] The frightening reality would actually take place as prophesied (chapter 1, verse 1). The Lord's power to convulse the land, so readily sung about in enthusiastic worship (chapter 9, verse 5), was actually going to happen.

❏ *The third sign of the end: a darkened sun (chapter 8, verses 9 and 10)*

Creation responded to the violation of the covenant. For Yahweh is the Lord also of creation. 'On that day', the day of Yahweh, the earth was to be covered in terrifying darkness (chapter 5, verses 18 to 20).

All the Bethel temple festivals that should lead to joy (feasts, singing) would only produce sadness (verse 10). Yahweh would make sure of this. All were to be marked by mourning (shaved heads, sackcloth). Weeping would be inconsolable on that bitter day (chapter 5, verses 16 and 17). This would be the end of all.

'I am the one doing this,' said Yahweh.

❑ *The fourth sign of the end: the absence of God's word (chapter 8, verses 11 and 12)*

Famine was a sign of God's anger against his people (chapter 4, verse 6ff). But this was a different famine. There would be no comforting word from God to ease these bitter days. But the people in their desperation were not really interested in revelation. Word from any god would do, as verse 14 suggests.

They had silenced the prophets (chapter 2, verses 11 and 12) and said Amos was only a treacherous babbler (chapter 7, verse 16b). Without true repentance, they were to wander aimlessly without any assuring word, taking a fitting punishment. They would stagger over the whole nation, discovering only that Yahweh was terrifyingly silent. The word they ignored in days of prosperity was now voiceless.

❑ *The fifth sign of the end: dire thirst (verses 13 and 14)*

There would be no help from God or any other gods on that momentous day. Physical and spiritual drought would be so severe that the strongest (young women and men) would give up on their own strength. They would cry out for a word from God. But in their dire confusion, but still clutching to their eccentric sophistication in religious tastes, they would take oaths of loyalty to deities worshipped in Samaria, Dan and Beersheba (verse 14).

Oaths like 'as Yahweh lives' usually enforced the truthfulness of a worshipper's vow. Here, it was perverted in the name of a god of Dan (northern Palestine), the place of syncretistic worship, where Jeroboam I had put one of his golden calves (1 Kings 12, verse 29). People at Beersheba, too, were calling on a god who had no power. Amos gave no clearer details, but focussed more specifically on corruptions in social relationships and on the economy (chapter 4, verses 1 to 3; chapter 6, verses 1 to 8).

There was no power to rise up from any of these false religious systems. Israel, too, was surely to fall and never rise again (chapter 5, verse 3).

VISION 5: The awesome Lord (chapter 9, verses 1 to 4)

This is the final vision. Amos was standing in the awesome presence of the Lord himself as he commanded destruction from the temple, the very place where the people expected refuge. This vision confirmed all the other visions, as well as underlining the prophet's authority. Amos was in intimate communication with the almighty Lord in his holy place.

There was no protection, mercy, blessing, joyful worship in this temple — only judgment, chaos and destruction as whole buildings tumbled down on the worshippers (verse 1). How hollow now were

The consequences of fractured relationships/163

their usual slogans of immunity: 'God is with us' (chapter 5, verse 14), 'Disaster will not overtake or meet us' (chapter 9, verse 10).

The chaotic scene demonstrates the power of a possible earthquake (chapter 9, verse 5). The corrupting influences of perverted worship,[9] which destroyed relationships with Yahweh for generations, had to end. The same destruction was meted out to Baal prophets and worshippers (2 Kings 10, verse 25). Those who lead others away from loving relationships with God, and those who followed, suffered the same terrifying judgment.

Flight would be useless. Those still alive would also be killed — probably by military invasion ('sword': verse 1). But Yahweh was the agent of destruction. Hiding from him was useless.

For a nation so secure, settled and prosperous, Yahweh as a sanctuary seemed superfluous. Amos therefore piled on extremes of locations as examples of the extent of his authority. These prove that nothing escaped Yahweh's majestic sovereignty in judgment:

* the grave or the heavens (verse 2 — compare with Psalm 139, verses 7 to 9)
* Mt Carmel (see chapter 1, verse 2) or the bottom of the sea (verse 3), where mystical serpents would only add to Yahweh's vengeance
* exile (verse 4), where further destruction

compounded the shame of losing their land,
God's precious covenant gift.

The people had despised his command to seek good and not evil (chapter 5, verses 14 and 15). Their injustice and corrupt worship showed in fact that they loved evil.

The awful stare of the mighty warrior would now only focus evil on them, not good (verse 4). The reversal of his favour was horrific. This is Yahweh's legal verdict on perverters of his covenant.

Hymn of praise to Yahweh (chapter 9, verses 5 and 6)

How could you feel like singing after that announcement? Other hymns (chapter 4, verse 13 and chapter 5, verses 8 and 9) might be seen as equally and powerfully inappropriate. Amos reminded the people that the God they worshipped in verses 5 and 6 was the same warrior God of judgment outlined in verses 1 to 4.

In this hymn, Yahweh is seen as the God who:

* touches the earth and it melts, so human strength dissolves and cries for mercy (chapter 5, verse 17)
* convulses the land (probably in an earthquake) so that it rises and sinks like the tides of the River Nile (chapter 8, verse 8)
* lives in heavenly splendour

* creates the earth
* controls the seas and rain.

The hymn glorifies the great majesty of Yahweh, the creator. Who can withstand his mighty power? Who is not terrified at his awesome strength? The prophet strained poetic hyperbole to describe his absolute majesty. *This* was Israel's God. He created every corner of the earth, the realm of the dead, the heavens, Mt Carmel, the sea. There is no place that is not under his authority. This is the Lord in action. But he will also judge.

Israel had no special moral privilege (chapter 9, verses 7 to 10)

Now Amos gave his strongest statement of Yahweh's rejection of his covenant people. Probably the audience continued to challenge the prophet's message of judgment on the basis of their cherished history of salvation. Amos' assault on their theology of election and deliverance is here complete. This is a radical interpretation of God's sovereignty to listeners used to assuming they could manipulate his promises.

Amos didn't deny the people's covenant relationship with Yahweh. He didn't belittle God's deliberate choosing them and his amazing intervention in their past salvation (chapter 3, verses 1 and 2). The issue is: the past blessings came in the context of loving relationships. They were not inviolable talismans to manipulate God into acting for them in the future.

Was Israel, then, no different from the Ethiopians to Yahweh (verse 7)? They were known to Israel as servants and eunuchs, strange and distant people. Such a comparison humiliated Israel. Then there were the twelfth century migrations of their bitter enemies — the Philistines (from 'Caphtor', Crete) and the Arameans (Syrians from Kir in Mesopotamia: see chapter 1, verse 5). Was God directing these as surely as he did the Israelites' escape from Egypt?

The Exodus had created Israel and given the people confidence in their freedom and future destiny. Here the prophet had the audacity to say that other national migrations had been under the same providence as the one who delivered the Israelites out of Egyptian slavery.

Amos made the issues very clear: Yahweh, their God, was also the God of the nations, acting in kindness as well as in judgment. The latter was easy to accept for others. Israelites also had no problems in seeing that past kindnesses guaranteed no other nations immunity from future danger. But Yahweh was to remain master of his own choices for Israel, too. His covenant relationship with Israel was unique because it demonstrated his universal goal through them. He set Israel free first in the Exodus in order to guarantee the liberation of all peoples (Genesis 12, verse 1ff).

Tragically, God argued, his relationship with Israel was in tatters at that moment. The nation had become a 'sinful kingdom' (verse 8). God's grace can never be seized as a weapon to be wielded at demand. It constantly calls for humble surrender. God's actions for his people at one point in history does not rule out the reality that he will later act against them if the relationship disintegrates. The God who gave them a past would not necessarily give them a future.

This word devastated Israel. By her disobedience she had forfeited all that her history entitled her to. This was the great tragedy of abused relationships.

These verses need to be handled carefully. Some scholars see in them the argument for different forms of universalism or pluralism — that God has been equally working for salvation in the history of other nations. Christopher Wright points out in this regard:

> But Amos did not say that the other nations were like Israel, but that Israel had become like *them*, in God's sight, because of their sinfulness and his imminent judgment.[10]

Amos affirmed God's sovereignty over other migrations but, continues Wright, these 'cannot mean that he believed that God had "redeemed" those nations through these events or that they stood in the same covenant relationship with God as Israel did.'[11]

Amos 3, verses 1 and 2 holds that Yahweh's relationship with Israel was exclusive. She was 'known' by God, but without any privileges to escape judgment. However, Israel's special covenant relationship did not detract from other truths in Amos: God was sovereignly active in other nations and his purposes were ultimately universal. Of this, Christopher Wright writes:

> What it comes down to is that, while God has every nation in view in his redemptive purpose, in no other nation did he act as he did in Israel: for the sake of the nations. That was their uniqueness, which can be seen to be both *exclusive* (in the sense that no other nation experienced what they did of God's revelation and redemption) and *inclusive* (in the sense that they were created, called and set in the midst of the nations for the sake of ultimately bringing salvation to the nations).[12]

Here God personally commanded the destruction of Israel (verse 9a). It would be thorough and extensive (verse 9b). He would use these other despised nations as his instruments.[13]

Sin was still the basis of judgment, no matter what the heritage or virtues of the nation. Those who sought him and did justice would live (chapter

5, verses 14 and 15). There would be a remnant: 'I will not totally destroy,' God said (verse 8b). The good grain would be sifted out (chapter 5, verse 3).

But judgment would be total for sinners — those who manipulated his promises for their own benefit (verse 10b) and those who flaunted their independence of Yahweh by their commitment to systems of evil. Past relationships — even eternal promises — are not licences for sin or guarantees of immunity from judgment. All peoples are accountable.

The eye of the sovereign Lord alone can pierce the heart and determine who are the sinners, as outward displays of religious fervour are so deceptive.

Discussion questions

Talking it through

1 What sort of relationship does this passage indicate that God had with Amos? What does this indicate:
(a) about how God works?
(b) about how prayer works?
(c) about what prayer is?
Do you find this encouraging?

2 What caused God to relent in chapter 7, verses 3 and 6? What does this indicate about God's view about:
(a) illusion and reality?
(b) weakness and strength?
(c) flexibility in the face of circumstances?

3 Amos, the 'amateur' prophet, had strong words to say to Amaziah, the official priest of the royal sanctuary of Bethel (chapter 7, verses 10 to 17).
(a) Why did God hold Amaziah so accountable for his actions? Why was he so

The consequences of fractured relationships/171

keen that Amos should simply disappear — 'buzz off' in colloquial terms (see verses 12 and 13)?

(b) Look at Amos' self-effacing description of himself (verses 14 and 15). He was not a member of a prophetic guild or 'band of prophets', yet God called him? What was the basis of Amos' sense of mission? Has this any application to recognition of non-authorised but valid forms of ministry in the church today, or are we simply talking about a different epoch with radically different circumstances?

4 What indications are there in chapter 8, verses 4 to 14 that the judgments were just? What modern parallels are there to the behaviour of the people of Israel as outlined here?

5 What was Israel's relationship with God, according to chapter 9, verses 7 to 10? Why was Israel as open to judgment as any other nation?

What principle is here about God's dealings with people in all ages?

Widening our horizons

1 What do you understand the nature of visions, such as Amos' here, to be? Is there a place for them today? If so, what role should they play in our lives?

Why do you think they are so infrequent?

2 Using chapter 9, verse 7 as a starting-point, what are the implications of God being the God of all nations for:
(a) our view of witness and evangelism in the world?
(b) our view of cultures different from ours?
(c) our view of God's judgment on nations today?

3 What is the value of vulnerability and weakness rather than 'strength' to Christians? Does strength and stability necessarily aid Christian witness? Use the following passage as a starting point for discussing there issues:

. . .each of the 462 missionaries comprising the Indian Evangelical Team serving in Northern India operates at an average monthly support level of $18. Missionaries from the Kachin Baptist Church in Burma do the work of an apostle for even less, serving six year terms throughout that region of Burma and in Yunan Province without any financial remittance whatsoever.

These missionaries, poor and lacking in training, have accomplished tremendous results, reporting 6550 conversions as a direct result of their evangelising in Yunan Province during the past four years. The growth and the effectiveness of financially and organisationally 'weak' non-Western mission agencies and missionaries far outstrips that of their Western counterparts. Despite their growing poverty (and its concomitant weakness) relative to the Western lands, even conservative projections estimate that, by the year 2000, most Christian missionaries will be from the Two-Thirds World.[14]

4 Contemporary preaching in most denominational circles has moved away from the notion of a God who judges to a God who accepts.
   (a) What are the sociological pressures (as distinct from theological ones) that have led to this development? What risks do we run in tailoring the gospel to contemporary need? What about 'seeker services'?
   (b) Where was God's judgment directed: to the people of God or the heathen around? What message, if any, is there in this for us? Where does God's judgment start?

8
Relationship restored

AMOS CHAPTER 9, VERSES 11 TO 15

LISTENERS WOULD HAVE BEEN LEFT EXHAUSTED; they would either have been challenged into brokenness and repentance or hardened into brazen rejection. There is no neutral ground for the people of God. They could trade no longer either on God's presence (chapter 5, verse 14) or on his protection. 'That day', the day of Yahweh, was a day of blighted hopes and destruction.[1]

This has been Amos' message. He has had to redress false hopes and securities about 'that day' based on self-assurance and manipulated theology.

Now Amos challenged his listeners to a radical reinterpretation of judgment. It was not the final word on failure but, as Walter Wink said, 'the first word on a new creation'.[2] As surely as 'that day' would bring destruction for the deceived (chapter 5, verses 18 to 20), it would fulfil all the most cherished promises of the faithful (chapter 9, verses 11 to 15). The promised blessings of 'the day of Yahweh', based on Yahweh's terms, would come. After the judgment, there would be restoring, rebuilding, renewing instead of 'falling' (chapter 5, verse 25; chapter 8, verse 14). The kingdom of David (verse 11) would be restored to its former glory. Amos here embraced both nations in these future blessings. After all the tragic divisions, these kingdoms would be reunited.

'Fallen tent' (verse 11) is a reminder of the Israelites' wandering in the wilderness and later building makeshift dwellings at the Feast of Booths in memory of their humble origins (Leviticus 23, verse 40). No longer would there be fortresses built to horde the gain of oppressing the poor and to parade human invincibility. They would be in ruins. But humble reliance on Yahweh, trusting his grace alone, would be the source of their pride and their relationship with their God.

'Broken places' (verse 11), or systems destroyed by perversions of justice and righteousness (chapter 4, verse 1), would be repaired as covenant priorities were re-established. This verse is attested by the Qumran texts, the Dead Sea scrolls of the Essene community. So Amos was read by the Essenes as a witness of the coming Messiah who would save Israel. Out of destruction comes hope.

The territory belonging to David's kingdom would be recovered (verse 12). Edom, with such a history of revenge and hatred towards Israel (chapter 1, verses 11 and 12), would be reincorporated peacefully, probably gratefully. Those of her people remaining after the judgment would also enjoy the blessings of the restored kingdom. The restoration had universal overtones. Similarly blessed would be those of other nations who had been faithful to Yahweh, on whom his name had been invoked as a sign of a special relationship ('called by my name': verse 12). Other nations would have equal access to the blessings.

James used an amended version of verses 11 and 12 to challenge the early church to open its hearts to Gentiles (Acts 15, verses 16 to 18). The rebuilt 'David's fallen tent' includes all others who seek the Lord. James resorted to Amos' universalistic perspective to resolve the contentious issue of the status of believers of non-Israelite origin in the church. Hundreds of years later, the people of God still struggled with the radical concept that it was *only* on the basis of love relationships, not status, race or heritage, that Yahweh could fulfil his promises to his creation.

Amos announced the destiny of a new Israel — the unity of believers of all nations who worship the only true God and demonstrate lives of justice and righteousness.

Curses (chapter 5, verse 11) on the land would also be reversed. No personal messiah is predicted, though it is significant that restoration is in relation to the house of David (verse 11). Blessings and curses were integral to the covenant: curses for those who breached the covenant; blessings for those who remained true to Yahweh (Leviticus 26, Deuteronomy 28). The return of these blessings was Yahweh's doing alone. Production would be so abundant (verse 13) that ploughers for the next crop would overtake those still attempting to harvest the previous one. Wines would flow down the hills. The Garden of Eden would be reborn. The new prosperity would be for everyone, affectionately called 'my exiled people' (verse 14), not just for the wealthy and powerful who had so greedily monopolised the benefits of God's gracious provisions at the expense of the poor.

The exile would be reversed (verse 14). Cities would not be any longer scenes of abject oppression and ostentation. Living would be full of purpose, where people could enjoy the rewards of their labour (chapter 2, verse 9; cf. Isaiah 65, verses 17 to 25). Human effort played an important part in this eschatological prosperity.

There would be peace without enemies dislocating them. God would do what he had said: he would be true to his covenant blessings. 'This is your God speaking', said Yahweh (verse 15). His grace is as powerful as his wrath (chapter 9, verses 1 to 10).

Yahweh closed by renewing his commitment to be to his people all he had promised. He alone could fulfil this. His judgment did not obliterate his promises. Yahweh was working towards the consummation of his covenant. It is the crowning expression of his sovereignty to restore his elect people to covenant relationships.

There is no reference, here, to the repentance required by Israel. As usual in Amos, the focus is on the sovereign Lord — the initiator, sustainer and healer of all relationships with his people. As Sine says:

> In the biblical vision, the initiative for change comes from neither humankind nor the natural order, but from the Creator God. It is God who is giving birth to a whole new order. And as we know, birth doesn't take place without a great deal of pain and trauma.[3]

God has expressed his pain through Amos: the pain of judging those he lovingly chose as his people. But out of the pain comes hope, the 'wild hope'[4] of rivers of justice and mighty streams of righteousness.

A final word:

> Although it is God who brings about God's future, we have a role to play as well. Our role

doesn't involve taking power, leveraging the market, or pursuing our own self-interest. It comes through relinquishing our own agendas and placing God's agenda first. It comes through suffering love and sometimes even through death. It comes through our cooperating with the Creator in the birthing of a whole new order.[5]

We live as people in anticipation that the Creator has the final say. Let us participate in sharing his pain, so this hope will become more of a reality where injustice and unrighteousness seem now to reign.

Discussion questions

Talking it through

1 Why is it appropriate in this section that *God* rather than the people should be the focus of attention? How does this seem to put the book in its proper perspective?

What does such an emphasis tell us about our own situation?

2 What effect do you think the knowledge that evil and injustice would come to an end have had on Amos' hearers? What effect should an absolute and unshakeable confidence in this truth have on our attitude today to:
(a) evils in our society and the sense that the forces of darkness overwhelm the church of God?
(b) people's failure to trust God, with a concomitant growth in superstition (such as astrology), paganism (such as pre-Christian folk religions) and the New Age/human potential movement?

Relationships restored/181

(c) increasing poverty and injustice to our world?

3 What is the role of human effort in bringing about the transformations promised in the day of the Lord (chapter 9, verse 14; see also Isaiah 61, verse 4; chapter 62, verse 8 and chapter 65, verse 21ff)?

How should this reality affect our interpretation of 2 Peter 3, verse 13: 'We wait for new heavens and a new earth, in which righteousness dwells'?

4 God's blessing is described in material terms: agricultural wealth, physical well-being, fortified cities, a self-sufficient agrarian lifestyle in which one enjoys the fruit of one's labour (verse 13 and 14).

Today, in our heavily urbanised societies, such a vision has a quaint or, at best, nostalgic appeal. Can you put Amos' description of the 'good life under God' into more contemporary terms?
(a) What for you will be the hallmark of 'God's new society' in which the Messiah will reign? What will be its greatest point of appeal?
(b) What are the spiritual, physical, cultural and sociological expressions of this kingdom?

Widening our horizons

1 The American civil rights leader, Martin Luther King, said:

> The storm is rising against the privileged minority of the earth, from which there is no shelter in isolation and armament. The storm will not abate until a just distribution of the fruits of the earth enables men everywhere to live in dignity and human decency.[6]

Do you think that the following are content with the present distribution of the earth's resources:
(a) those who are better off in the Western world?
(b) those who are worse off in the Third World?

How is this situation likely to resolve itself? In an ideal world, what should be done? What *can* be done in the real world? Do we see any sign of God's judgment here?

2 German theologian, Walter Brueggemann, says:

> The task of prophecy is to empower people to engage in history.[7]

Is that your evaluation of prophecy? If so, how does it do this?

3 Write some conclusions on your response to Amos. Add to or modify these:

Our covenant privileges must be enjoyed with humility, since Yahweh cares for and commands the destinies of all peoples, even our enemies.

Our sense of security must be anchored in God alone, since our days of prosperity and blessing — and our times of austerity — may be his discipline.

Our worship must motivate and inform our acts of righteousness and justice towards all humanity, especially the poor, afflicted and oppressed.

Our piety must have one essential aim (and one vital test of validity): the emulation of the One whom we adore, the One who has shown himself to be ultimate righteousness and justice, final truth and grace: Jesus Christ.

If we are feeling overwhelmed by the cynicism of society to the gospel and the strength of the opposition, remember: God is in charge. Victory lies with the One who oversees the fate of nations.

4 What action has Amos stirred you to make in your:
  (a) personal life?
  (b) public life (social, political and economic)?
  (c) international commitments?

  How can you be part of the torrent of justice and righteousness God longs for?

5 How can we be part of creating a new order? Are there any clues from this quote?

> Christ's method of dealing with evil must be our method also — we must be ready to absorb all that the powers of evil can do to us, and to neutralise it with forgiving love. 'Be not outwardly conformed to this age, but be transformed by the renewing of your mind — recompense no man evil for evil — avenge not yourself, but give place to wrath — if your enemy is hungry feed him; if he is thirsty give him drink. Do not be overcome by evil, but overcome evil with good.' Any other method of meeting evil means being conformed to this present age, which is under the domination of the principalities and powers. Any other method of meeting evil means being severed from Christ. Any other method of meeting evil is a reversion to the weak, beggarly elements from whose bondage Christ has set us free.[8]

Endnotes

Preface
1. Tom Sine, *Wild Hope*, Monarch, 1991, p.248
2. Walter Wink, *Engaging the Powers: Discernment and Resistance in a World of Domination*, Fortress, 1992, p.308

Introduction
1. Gerhard F. Hasel, *Understanding the Book of Amos: Basic Issues in Current Interpretations*, Baker, 1991, p.26
2. John Perkins, address to Aboriginal Evangelical Fellowship, Port Augusta, South Australia, 1984
3. Walter Wink, *op.cit.*, p.16
4. Ephesians 6, verse 12
5. Alexander Solzhenitzen, in Roy Clements, *Where Love and Justice Meet: The Truth of Amos for Today*, IVP, 1988
6. Austin Donnelly, The *Courier Mail*, 2 January, 1993
7. *Newsweek*, December 1992, pp. 106-107

Chapter 1

1. Walter Brueggemann, *The Prophetic Imagination*, Fortress, 1973, p.13
2. *Ibid*, p.41
3. 'Down and Out in Paradise', The *Courier Mail*, 16 January, 1993

Chapter 2

1. Thomas Shapcott, in *Anthology of Australian Religious Poetry*, Les A. Murray (ed.), Collins Dove, pp.37-38
2. Walter Wink, *op.cit.*, pp.205-206
3. *Ibid*, p.88
4. James Luther Mays, *Amos: A Commentary*, SCM, 1969, p.31
5. J.A. Motyer, *Summary of the Message of Amos*, Inter-Varsity Press, 1974, pp.35-47
6. David Hubbard, *Joel and Amos: An Introduction and Commentary*, Inter-Varsity Press, 1989, p.140
7. Wink, *op.cit.*, p.116
8. Hubbard, *op.cit.*, p.138
9. R. Martin-Achard and Re'emi S. Paul, *God's People in Crisis: A Commentary on the Books of Amos and Lamentations*, Eerdmans, 1984, p.23
10. James Mays, *op.cit.*, p.47
11. Walter Wink, *op.cit.*, p.30
12. John Smith, *The Heart of the Matter*, Commencement Address, University of Queensland, 21 March 1993
13. Bruce Wilson, 'Communicating the Gospel in Australia Today', *Interchange*, No.19, 1976, p.147
14. *Time*, 21 June 1993
15. The *Manila Chronicle*, 1 July, 1990
16. From *The Sheep and the Goats*. Background video notes. World Vision.

Chapter 3

1. P.J. Hartigan ('John O'Brien'), in Les A. Murray (ed.), *op.cit.*, pp.233-235
2. Walter Brueggemann, *op.cit.*, p.49
3. Gary V. Smith, *Amos: A Commentary*, Regency Reference Library, 1989, p.97
4. James Mays, *op.cit.*, p.158
5. Gary Smith, *op.cit.*, p.112
6. David Hubbard, *op.cit.*, p.153
7. Gerd Behrens, 'The Resistable Rise of the West', *Time*, 25 October 1993, p.56
8. Walter Wink, *op.cit.*, p.30
9. Walter Brueggemann, *op.cit.*, p.11
10. Rahab Ministry, Servants to Asia's Urban Poor, Bangkok

Chapter 4

1. In Les A. Murray (ed.), *op.cit.*, pp.13-14
2. St Basil, in *Common Wealth and Common Good*, Bishops' Conference for Justice, Development and Peace, Collins Dove, 1991, p.65
3. Gary V. Smith, *op.cit.*, p.149
4. James Mays, *op.cit.*, p.76
5. Jacques Ellul, *The Subversion of Christianity*, Eerdmans, 1986, pp.23-24
6. David Hubbard, *op.cit.*, p.158
7. Tom Sine, *op.cit.*, p.236
8. Walter Brueggeman, *op.cit.*, p.25
9. Walter Wink, *op.cit.*, p.167
10. *Ibid*
11. Walter Brueggemann, *op.cit.*, pp.25-27
12. Gailyn van Rheenen, 'Cultural Conceptions of Power in Biblical Perspective', *Missiology*, Vol.XXI, No.1, January 1993, p.49

13. *Ibid*, p.51
14. Roy Clements, *op.cit.*, p.62

Chapter 5

1. *Ibid*, p.51
2. *Ibid*, p.59
3. James Mays, *op.cit.*, p.85
4. *The Faith that Does Justice*, John C. Haughey (ed.), Paulist Press, 1977, p.69
5. James Mays, *op.cit.*, p.92
6. Stephen Charles Mott, *Biblical Ethics and Social Change*, Oxford University Press, 1982, p.66
7. Walter Wink, *op.cit.*, p.30
8. David Hubbard, *op.cit.*, p.173
9. Robert McAfee Brown, *Unexpected News: Reading the Bible with Third World Eyes*, Westminster, 1984, p.155

Chapter 6

1. Geoffrey B. Kelly, 'Cry Faithfulness', *The Other Side*, September-October, 1992, p.59
2. Servants to Asia's Urban Poor, Manila

Chapter 7

1. Kenneth Leech, *The Eye of the Storm: Spiritual Resources for the Pursuit of Justice*, Darton, Longman and Todd, 1992, p.174
2. Chapter 1, verses 4, 7, 10, 12 and 14; chapter 2, verses 2 and 5; chapter 5, verse 6
3. Walter Wink, *op.cit.*, p.297
4. cf. Exodus 3, verse 10 and Deuteronomy 4, verse 20
5. Chapter 4, verses 2 and 3; chapter 5, verse 27; chapter 6, verse 7; chapter 7, verse 17; chapter 9, verse 4
6. Chapter 3, verse 1; chapter 4, verse 1; chapter 5, verse 1;

chapter 7, verse 16
7. Chapter 2, verse 12; chapter 4, verse 1; chapter 5, verse 14; chapter 6 verses 2 and 13; chapter 8, verse 14; chapter 9, verse 10
8. Chapter 2, verse 13; chapter 3, verses 14 and 15; chapter 9, verse 1
9. Chapter 2, verse 8; chapter 4, verses 4 and 5 and 21 to 26; chapter 8, verse 14
10. Christopher J.H. Wright, *Knowing Jesus through the Old Testament*, Marshall Pickering, 1993, p.42
11. *Ibid*
12. *Ibid*, p.43
13. Chapter 3, verses 11 and 12; chapter 4, verses 2 and 3; chapter 5, verse 27; chapter 6, verse 7; chapter 7, verse 17; chapter 9, verse 4
14. Jonathon J. Bonk, 'Small is (Still) Beautiful in Missions', in *Transformation*, January/March 1992, p.26

Chapter 8

1. Chapter 3, verse 14; chapter 4, verse 2; chapter 6, verse 3; chapter 8, verses 3, 9, 11 and 13
2. Walter Wink, *op.cit*, p.266
3. Tom Sine, *op.cit.*, p.253
4. Tom Sine's book title, *op.cit.*
5. Tom Sine, *op.cit.*, p.253
6. Kenneth Leech, *op.cit.*, p.231
7. Walter Brueggemann, *op.cit.*, p.22
8. G.B. Baird, *Principalities and Powers: A Study in Pauline Theology*, Clarendon, 1956, p.100, in Tom Sine, *op.cit.*, p.254

Bibliography

Useful commentaries on Amos

R. Martin-Achard and Re'emi S. Paul, *God's People in Crisis: A Commentary on the Books of Amos and Lamentations*, Eerdmans, 1984
Part of the International Theological Commentary Series, this commentary is addressed to ministers and Christian educators, and has a critical-historical approach as well as theological interpretation.

Francis L. Anderson and David Noel Freedman, *Amos*, The Anchor Bible, Doubleday, 1989
An expansive, scholarly treatment, including recent critical research.

Roy Clements, *Where Love and Justice Meet: The Truth of Amos for Today*, IVP, 1988
A series of ten sermons which sees Amos' modern relevance as addressing social evils in the nation, rebuking apostasy in the church and challenging individuals

to repentance. It asks readers to identify as the prophet's original audience.

Robert B. Coote, *Amos Among the Prophets*, Fortress, 1981
Describes the gradual stages of formation of Amos: oral legacy, theological import, understanding pre-exilic prophecy and comparisons with other prophetic traditions.

D. David Garland, *Amos*, Lamplighter Books, 1966
A brief, non-critical, thematic approach.

John H. Hayes, *Amos, The Eighth-Century Prophet: His Times and His Preaching*, Abingdon, 1988
A comprehensive commentary, including recent issues of scholarly research on Amos.

David Allan Hubbard, *Joel and Amos: An Introduction and Commentary*, IVP, 1989
A thorough treatment of questions, original setting and main themes, combining scholarship with a respect for the text. In the Tyndale series of Old Testament commentaries.

James Luther Mays, *Amos: A Commentary*, SCM, 1969
Written for use by ministers and theological students in the interpretation and understanding of scripture.

Henry Mckeating, *Amos, Hosea, Micah*, Cambridge University Press, 1971
Discusses chronology, structure and contents and shows how these three prophets are alike in their intensity, reflecting three different attitudes to a corrupt society.

J.A. Motyer, *The Message of Amos*, IVP, 1974
In 'The Bible Speaks Today' series, it focusses on applying the exposition to contemporary life.

Gary V. Smith, *Amos: A Commentary*, Regency Reference Library, 1989
Presents a non-defensive evangelical perspective on issues of textual criticism, structure, historical and literary background, unity and theological significance of the text. In the Library of Biblical Interpretation Series.

J. Alberto Soggin, *The Prophet Amos*, SCM, 1987
A translation from the Hebrew, giving reasons for the translation and an historical and exegetical commentary.

Bernard Thorogood, *A Guide to the Book of Amos*, SPCK, 1987
A student's guide giving historical background, summary of the prophet's message, notes on particular verses and study suggestions.

Useful investigations of the key ideas in Amos

Robert McAfee Brown, *Unexpected news. Reading the Bible with Third World Eyes*, Westminster Press, 1984
The author uses stories and reflections from the Third World to challenge us with the notion that the world of the Bible is a more accurate view of the world than our own.

Gerhard F. Hasel, *Understanding the Book of Amos: Basic Issues in Current Interpretation*, Baker, 1991

A summary of scholarship over the last thirty years, with a most extensive bibliography.

Tom Sine, *Wild Hope*, Monarch, 1991

An incisive assessment of future trends and assumptions underlying Christians' responses. A reminder of the biblical foundation of hope and the spiritual authority to proclaim it.

Christopher J.H. Wright, *Knowing Jesus through the Old Testament*, Marshall Pickering, 1993

Traces the authenticity and centrality of Jesus through to Old Testament scriptures.

Useful treatments of present-day faith and life issues raised in Amos

AD 2000 and Beyond: A Mission Agenda, Vinay Samuel and Chris Sudgen (eds), Regnum, 1991

An international collection of essays reflecting on the theology and holistic missiology of the future church.

Walter Brueggemann, *The Prophetic Imagination*, Fortress, 1978

Brueggemann's hypothesis is this: 'The task of prophetic ministry is to nurture, nourish and evoke a consciousness and perception alternative to the consciousness and perception of the dominant culture around us.' A clear understanding of prophetic ministry, combining its rich Old Testament heritage, the prophetic ministry of Jesus and current implications.

The Church in Response to Human Need, Vinay Samuel and Chris Sugden (eds), Regnum, 1987
Papers from the 1983 Wheaton Consultation on the church's relationship to social development.

Jaques Ellul, *Money and Power*, IVP, 1984
Traces scriptural attitudes towards wealth and challenges Christians to live by the law of grace and not the law of the marketplace.

Jaques Ellul, *The Subversion of Christianity*, Eerdmans, 1986
Challenges the divorce between modern Christianity and the 'scandal' of the revelation of God.

The Faith That Does Justice: Examining the Christian Resources for Social Change, John C. Haughey (ed.), Paulist Press, 1977
Occasional papers (Vol.2) from the Jesuit Woodstock Theological Centre which examine the relationship of justice issues to the practical faith of Christians in society.

Jim Halteman, *Market Capitalism and Christianity*, Baker, 1988
Evaluates current economic behaviour in the light of biblical teaching.

Kenneth Leech, *The Eye of the Storm: Spiritual Resources for the Pursuit of Justice*, Darton, Longman and Todd, 1992

Leech examines the link between spirituality and human liberation, the need for a fresh vision in social action, and the unity of contemplation and action.

Mission as Witness and Justice: An Indian Perspective, Bruce Nicholls and Christopher Raj (eds), TRACI, 1991

Herbert Schlossberg, *Idols for Destruction*, Crossway, 1990
Examines the conflict of Christian faith and American culture.

Keith Suter, *Global Change: Armageddon and the New World Order*, Albatross, 1992
Examines current global events in the light of debate about the picture of human society.

John White, *Money Isn't God, So Why is the Church Worshipping It?*, IVP, 1993
The author challenges the Western church with idolatry and calls for repentance.

John Wilson, *The Old Testament and Christian Living*, Anglican Information Office, 1981
Ten Old Testament themes and their relevance to today's issues. Amos chapter 5 is covered in the chapter, 'Justice is not an optional extra.'

Walter Wink, *Engaging the Powers: Discernment and Resistance in a World of Domination*, Fortress, 1992
Examines the spiritual powers behind modern crises

and offers insights on how these can be engaged and resisted. Highly acclaimed treatment of the biblical and contemporary meaning of the powers. The third volume in his trilogy which includes *Naming the Powers* (1984) and *Unmasking the Powers* (1986).

Notes

Notes

Notes

Notes

Notes

Notes

Notes

Notes

Notes

Notes